"Fresh, helpful, exciting!"

"I know no one better positioned to address this significant theme of effective, biblical stewardship than my beloved friend, Bill Bright. His teaching on the art, the gift and joy of stewardship is fresh, exceedingly helpful and genuinely exciting. Bright helps us to understand, in a new and fresh way, the utter delight of Christian obedience. This practical, applicable book in no way is threatening, but helpfully releasing."

Ted W. Engstrom, President Emeritus
World Vision

"How helped I was through reading Bill's new book. I have been in stewardship work for many years, and have always been impressed with two primary things:

— how beautifully God provides for Christian work
— how beautifully God blesses faithful stewards

"This is a book which should be read by all growing Christians."

E. Brandt Gustavson, Executive Vice-President
Trans World Radio

"*As You Sow* is warm, inspirational, practical and transferable. Christians will find it useful in their individual study, or in group settings such as Sunday school or home Bible studies."

William L. McConkey, President
Development Association for Christian
Institutions

"I highly commend this book on Christian stewardship to the Christian who seriously wants to explore his relationship to God within the framework of his life, his abilities, and his financial resources.

"Many facets of Christian stewardship are explored from a biblical perspective and illustrated within the life experiences of those who dared to take God at His Word."

Marvin McLean, Regional Representative
Department of Stewardship
Moody Bible Institute

Also by Bill Bright

The Secret: How to Live With Purpose and Power

Witnessing Without Fear
(Winner of the 1988 Gold Medallion Award)

Promises: A Daily Guide to Supernatural Living

Have You Heard of the Four Spiritual Laws?

Would You Like to Know God Personally?

Have You Made the Wonderful Discovery
of the Spirit-filled Life?

Kingdoms at War

A Handbook for Christian Maturity

The Holy Spirit: Key to Supernatural Living

The Transferable Concepts

Transferable Concepts for Powerful Living

Ten Basic Steps to Christian Maturity

Five Steps to Christian Growth

Come Help Change the World

Revolution Now!

As You Sow

Bill Bright

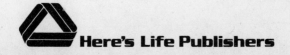
Here's Life Publishers

First printing, September 1989

Published by
HERE'S LIFE PUBLISHERS, INC.
P. O. Box 1576
San Bernardino, CA 92402

Library of Congress Cataloging-in-Publication Data
Bright, Bill.
    As you sow — : the adventure of giving by faith / Bill Bright.
       p.   cm.
    ISBN 0-89840-262-X
    1. Christian giving.   2. Stewardship, Christian.   I. Title.
    BV772.B72   1989
    248'.6 — dc 20   89-36763
    CIP

For More Information, Write:
L.I.F.E. — P.O. Box A399, Sydney South 2000, Australia
Campus Crusade for Christ of Canada — Box 300, Vancouver, B.C., V6C 2X3, Canada
Campus Crusade for Christ — Pearl Assurance House, 4 Temple Row, Birmingham, B2 5HG, England
Lay Institute for Evangelism — P.O. Box 8786, Auckland 3, New Zealand
Campus Crusade for Christ — P.O. Box 240, Colombo Court Post Office, Singapore 9117
Great Commission Movement of Nigeria — P.O. Box 500, Jos, Plateau State Nigeria, West Africa
Campus Crusade for Christ International — Arrowhead Springs, San Bernardino, CA 92414, U.S.A.

Contents

Acknowledgments 7

Part 1: Called to Stewardship

1. Stewards Over All 11

2. Blessings of Stewardship 19

3. Qualifications of a Steward 29

4. Attitudes of a Steward 41

5. Responsibilities of a Steward 49

Part 2: Keys to God's Abundant Blessings

6. The Principles of Giving 61

7. The Basis of Giving 73

8. The Goal of Giving 81

9. Motives for Giving 93

Part 3: God's Plan for Systematic Giving

10. Tithing: Addressing the Controversy . . . 109

11. Tithing: The Historical Foundation 117

12. Tithing in a Modern World 131

13. Tithing Your Time and Talents 139

Part 4: Steps to Financial Freedom

14. God Wants Us to Be Financially Free . . . 151

15. How to Be Financially Free 163

16. "Give While Your Hand Is Warm" 175

17. How to Trust God for Your Finances . . . 183

18. The Adventure of Giving by Faith 195

Appendix A: How to Help
Change Your World 207

Appendix B: Resources to Help You Grow
and Share Your Faith 213

Notes 217

Acknowledgments

Right now, I am enjoying one of the most exciting adventures in ministry of my lifetime. In cooperation with millions of Christians from thousands of churches of all denominations and hundreds of mission organizations, Campus Crusade is leading a comprehensive strategy for evangelism and discipleship called New Life 2000.

The goal of New Life 2000 is to help present the gospel of our Lord Jesus Christ to more than six billion people by the year 2000. On the basis of our current experience, we estimate that more than a billion will make salvation decisions. As a result, a million new churches will be established.

In light of this, I have a great desire to teach new Christians the biblical basis of giving. I also want to encourage them to become faithful stewards of their time, talent and treasure.

Through the years I have written many books and hundreds of articles. In the beginning of my ministry, I personally researched, wrote, edited and polished each book manuscript and article. Today, however, my responsibilities of leading a large worldwide movement and my appointments and travel schedule do not allow me such luxury.

So I happily sought the help of my good friend and Director of Editorial Projects, Don Tanner.

Don has helped me put into this book the essence of what I have sought to live and some of what I have taught for almost forty years. I am indebted to him for his professional assistance in helping to prepare this manuscript.

I thank Joette Whims for her extensive and thorough research in developing this book and for joining Don and me in the editorial process.

I also thank Barbara Fagan for her valuable contribution in research.

Part 1

Called to Stewardship

1

Stewards Over All

Deborah was a missionary serving overseas. Not long after her arrival back in the United States for her scheduled home leave, she learned that one of her neighbor's sons had been seriously injured. The family had no insurance and was suffering financially as well as physically.

Concerned about the situation, Deborah went into her bedroom to pray. "Lord," she asked, "what would you have me do?" She sensed a nudge from the Lord to give her neighbors some money. Checking her bank account, she realized that her bank balance was a mere $200.

"Lord, how about $25?" she prayed. With $175 left over, she thought she could survive the rest of the month. Quietly waiting on the Lord, however, she felt the Lord say, "No, I want you to give $100."

"I choked a bit," she says. "That was half of what I had. As I continued to question the Lord, I had no peace about anything less than $100."

Finally, she wrote out a check, breathing a prayer. "Now I've done what You said, so You'll have to take care of my needs."

With a sense of joy and expectancy, Deborah took the check across the street. By this act of sharing, she greatly encouraged the family, and God kept His word. Two days later a check for $100 came in the mail. Three days later a woman dropped by her home with a check for $200 — something she had wanted to do for some time, she told Deborah.

"Within five days of writing my check, I received from unexpected sources a total of $500," Deborah says. "I stood in awe of God and His ways."

Deborah discovered one of the greatest privileges and blessings of the Christian life — the wonderful adventure of giving by faith.

Throughout the Scripture, God promises us prosperity and abundance as we share that which He has given to us.

The Importance of Stewardship

Stewardship of what God has given us requires an understanding of our role in His economy.

A young boy put it well when he responded to a question on the meaning of stewardship. "It means that life is a ship loaded with a cargo of many things on its way to many people in many places," he said. "God is the Owner, but I am the captain of the ship, and He holds me responsible for the distribution."

In the New Testament, two different words describe a steward. One emphasizes guardianship over children and the administration of a master's household. The other stresses the role of a manager over property. In either case, a steward oversees the affairs and property of another person.

Not many of us have the resources to appoint a

steward over our affairs, so we are personally responsible. The decisions we make every day about spending and saving determine our effectiveness.

The average Christian is, however, ignorant of the basic principles of stewardship, and popular teachings about money are misleading many sincere believers. As a result, the kingdom of God is losing vast sums of money and other valuable resources, which could help change lives by the power of the risen Christ. The basic premise of this book is that most of what we give to the work of the Lord should have some relationship to fulfilling our Lord's Great Commission to "Go into all the world and preach the Good News to everyone, everywhere."[1] My goal is to help you discover how to invest wisely in God's kingdom and increase your fruitfulness for Christ.

Understanding Biblical Principles

We do not need to operate blindly or from ignorance in managing our stewardship. God has established principles valid for all time. I would like to help new Christians understand the biblical basis for stewardship and to bring balance to the practice of giving. I want Christians to see how they can experience the abundant life assured by God's promised blessings if we follow those principles for giving. Finally, I want to encourage Christians to help fulfill the Great Commission by investing strategically and generously in the expansion of the kingdom of God.

When we do not follow these biblical principles, financial disaster lies ahead. One of the first questions that comes to my mind when I am counseling a person who has financial problems is, "Are you obeying the laws of God concerning stewardship?" I'm convinced that these laws of God in the spiritual realm are as inviolate as the laws of the physical world. Ignorance of or disobedience to these laws results in all kinds of self-imposed poverty—materially and spiritually. The person who disobeys God in stewardship cannot walk in the fullness and power of the Holy Spirit. Neither can he know the joy of the Lord and the peace of Christ in his heart. The one who truly does what God tells him to do will experience the abundant life.

I'm sure all of us would like to experience true abundance. It's available! Our Lord said, "My purpose is to give life in all its fullness."[2] The apostle John records, "I pray that in all respects you may prosper and be in good health, just as your soul prospers."[3] Psalm 1 says that if we delight ourselves in the Lord, meditate upon His Word day and night, and always seek ways to follow Him more closely, we are like trees along a riverbank bearing luscious fruit each season without fail. Our leaves will never wither, and all we do will prosper.[4] However, prosperity and our role as keepers of God's blessings frequently have been misunderstood.

Few people realize that Jesus had much to say about money—more than virtually any other subject. We need to learn what He taught us! Yet our responsibility as stewards extends beyond the administration of finances. Stewardship over *all* that God entrusts to us in life is foundational to giving. Our task, then, is to manage our time and talent, as well as our treasure, to bring glory to His name.

All that we have, we own under God. Everything belongs to Him. He has never given us the absolute proprietorship in anything. The psalmist records, "The earth is the Lord's, and everything in it, the world, and all who live in it."[5] Jesus Christ created us.[6] He bought us with His precious blood.[7] God anointed Him as Lord.[8] God's ownership is eternal and unchanging. He never has given up this right—and never will.

Most Christians give only intellectual assent to this principle. Sometime ago a young man who was very egotistic came to tell me that he had problems of pride. "I find myself on my knees asking the Lord to make me humble," he confided. He thought he was a gifted speaker and that he had a marvelous singing voice. Frankly, I wasn't as impressed with him as he was with himself.

"God gives and God takes away. Everything is in the hands of the Lord to do with as He wishes," I counseled. "Suppose you have a heart attack and die. What would happen to your gifts then?"

The young man sobered. He had never really looked at life that way. The Scripture clearly teaches, "Do not think of yourself more highly than you ought, but rather think of yourself with sober judgment, in accordance with the measure of faith God has given you."[9]

What happens if I do not understand the spiritual principle of total stewardship and God's ownership over all that I am and what I possess? I could become enamored with my own importance. I could lose sight of the grace of God and think that through my own efforts I could become someone pretty special.

Those of us in public ministry sometimes forget who gives us everything we have. Everywhere I go, for example, people come to me with testimonies of how they found the Lord through my ministry or a member of our Campus Crusade staff. Frequently when I'm speaking in a church people gather around me after my message to say how their lives had changed through the ministry. Occasionally when I am on a plane, three or four passengers will relate how Christ has touched their lives through Campus Crusade. I could easily accept this praise personally. Yet God, in His grace, has anointed me and called me to be His servant. He does not share His glory with man. If I ever forget this, He will withdraw that blessing.

Foundational to all understanding of stewardship is

that God entrusts us with the responsibilities of His kingdom. He has put into our hands the administration of all that He owns. The Christian steward realizes that in Christ "we live and move and have our being."[10] God is our preeminent Master. The whole of our life — our personality, influence, material substance, everything — is His, even our successes. He holds us accountable for how we manage what He has given us.[11]

This divine perspective helps us understand our purpose for living as Christians. Apart from the command to love God and others, His most important command is to "Go into all the world" and "make disciples in all nations."[12] I am not here merely to enjoy the good life. I am here as a child and a servant of God to invest my time, my talent, and my treasure to seek and to save the lost. This is what our Lord came to do nearly 2,000 years ago, and what He commanded His followers to do generation after generation until His blessed return.

How to Get the Most Out of This Book

Read this book prayerfully. The only way to discern spiritual truth is to be sure your mind is controlled by the Holy Spirit. As you read this book, examine your heart for any unconfessed sin in your life. Be certain you are controlled and empowered by the Holy Spirit. Ask God to enable your mind to grasp these important biblical principles that could result in a revolutionary, supernatural lifestyle.

Study this book carefully, underlining significant points and making notes in the margins for quick, easy reference. The Scripture teaches that as a man thinks in his heart, so is he.[13] Learn the principles set forth in this book. Meditate on their application in your life so they will become a part of your lifestyle. To study this material without applying its principles is not a profitable stewardship of one's time. Read each chapter with careful attention to the suggested action points. In the process, the truths will become more indelibly impressed upon your mind.

Encourage your spouse to study with you. He or she has a legitimate claim on the family finances. Before making a commitment to stewardship, share that commitment with your mate.

Finally, share these principles with those whom you are discipling. Stewardship is a "transferrable concept" — a truth which can be transferred from one person to another, spiritual generation after generation, without distorting or diluting its original meaning. The apostle Paul encouraged Timothy to "teach others those things you and many others have heard me speak about . . . to trustworthy men who will, in turn, pass them on to others."[14] It is not enough for you to learn these principles for yourself. In the spirit of our Lord's Great Commission and the teaching of Paul, think of the individuals with whom you would like to share these truths.

I encourage you to master each of the principles until you can personally communicate them to those "who will, in turn, pass them on to others." In so doing, you will help disciple many men and women for Christ who will make a significant contribution toward fulfilling the Great Commission in our generation.

2

The Blessings of Stewardship

What does the word "adventure" mean to you?

Is it shooting the rapids on a hot summer day . . .

Or speeding around a race track at two hundred miles per hour . . .

Or climbing a sheer cliff in the Alps . . .

Or trekking through a wilderness on safari?

Most people don't relate adventure to the act of giving. In the coming pages I want to share with you a perspective on giving that can turn your stewardship into an exciting personal adventure. But first, let me tell you about some of God's children who have made this wonderful discovery.

Great Joy in Giving

A Christian businessman and his wife wrote to me recently, "One morning in the summer of 1971, the phone rang and a young couple from a major Christian ministry wanted an appointment to share their need for support. At that time our new recreational vehicle business kept us very busy. Appointments were hard to make and keep because of so many interruptions. We decided the best time to meet would be right after lunch.

"During the morning, we didn't have time to discuss what we should give. But, as in many times before, God spoke to each of us, planting the same figure in our minds — $650 a year. The amount was one-month's support at that time. The couple left feeling deeply grateful, and we went on being busy.

"At that time we were overcrowded at our location. A move to a better site would be expensive and could mean financial disaster for our young business.

"That evening after the couple left, my wife and I went to look at sixteen acres of property next to the exit of the Interstate. Tired of paying taxes on the land, the owner was willing to sell it for only a few thousand dollars. There is no doubt in our minds that because of our step of faith, God almost *gave* us this choice property.

"We have been able to continue this couple's support for the past seventeen years, even though monthly support has gone up to more than $3,500. We also help support two other missionary families.

"One year a friend needed a Land Rover for his missionary work in Africa. In the fall of the year, the RV business slows down, but we promised him we would have the money when he needed it. We get one big sales splash at our State Fair, where we usually sell about fifteen RVs — and that's good. That year, however, God rewarded our step of faith in pledging the vehicle by doubling our sales.

"We give because so many must hear about Jesus and how He can change their lives. There is real joy in giving!"

God Multiplies Events and Choices

Sam and Sarah learned that God multiplies even

trivial events and choices when we direct them toward Him.

For several years Sarah had wanted a beautiful new bedroom set. One day she saw the bed of her dreams—a copy of a colonial antique. Knowing how much she admired the furniture, Sam suggested that she order it.

Excitedly, she took the phone number and the catalog of the furniture company with her to church where she worked as a secretary. Before calling the furniture company, Sarah showed pictures of her selection to their pastor.

"My wife doesn't have such expensive taste," he mumbled. "But there's nothing wrong with buying it, if you have prayed about it."

His response changed Sarah's thinking. "Knowing I hadn't even considered praying about it," she says, "I immediately knew I should not make the extravagant purchase. For my 'sacrifice' to serve a good purpose, I decided to give the money we would have spent on the furniture to a friend, Dennis, who is on staff with Campus Crusade for Christ.

Sam and Sarah had not talked with Dennis in months, but the decision to send him the money led Sam to call him. During their conversation, Dennis urged Sam and Sarah to attend a nearby Family Life Conference where he would be speaking.

At the conference, Sam mentioned to Dennis his plan to take early retirement in ten years and go into full time Christian work. Dennis enthusiastically challenged Sam to examine the Family Ministry. At that time, Sam had no intention of joining Campus Crusade then or ever—not *then* because he had two daughters to put through college, and not *ever* because the idea of raising his own financial support was more than he could swallow.

The Lord took Sam and Sarah through a series of events which prepared their hearts and led Sam to resign his responsible and lucrative position with a major corporation to join staff. God provided miraculously with unexpected funds for their daughters' college expenses, an improved early retirement benefit and a quick sale of their home. He gave Sam and Sarah the confidence to walk away from financial security. He also provided them with a loyal support team in time to report to the Family Ministry two years later.

"We 'sowed' a little furniture money and are continuing to reap great riches from God," Sarah says. "We feel happier, more challenged and fulfilled. God consistently proves Himself faithful and sufficient. Furthermore, He has given us greater opportunities to influence those in our church and neighborhood."

God Delights in Giving to His Children

In August of 1985, God impressed Susan with the financial needs of the worldwide mission field. She had given occasionally in the past; now she saw the necessity of giving on a regular basis. The amount which she felt led to give was beyond her budget, but she gladly gave it anyway.

During a short missionary trip to Haiti the following January, Susan felt called of the Lord to become a nurse on the mission field. At first, all the necessary plans quickly fell into place. In preparation, she quit her job and enrolled full time in school. One night, less than two weeks before her first day of class, she discovered she needed $400 within three days to meet school expenses. Considering the things she would have to give up to cover the expenses and make a necessary lifestyle change, she felt bewildered and angry. *Why would the Lord provide so richly up to a point, then allow me to fail before I actually start?* she wondered.

Weighted down with sadness, she didn't feel like praying. "But I knew I had to give this anger to God," she says. "I confessed my attitude, asking Him to change it. And I thanked Him for being the Lord who loves and remains in control, even when I can't feel it."

God did change Susan's attitude, and during work the next day a friend approached her desk and handed her a card. A Christian less than six months, the friend had written the words, "God spoke to me concerning you last night," and enclosed a check for $375.

"Not even twenty-four hours had passed since I'd discovered my financial need," Susan says. "And here was Christ's speedy answer. Now, two years later, I cannot recall a single situation in which He hasn't met my needs, material or otherwise. I've learned that I just cannot outgive God, whether it's in time commitment, finances, or the stewardship of abilities. My unmerited reward is that I have a Father who delights in giving good gifts to His children."

Exciting to See How God Provides

Tom and Brenda have seen God work miracle after miracle with their finances since they became Christians in 1974 and decided to trust Him with their stewardship.

On one occasion, Dr. Joon Gon Kim, director of affairs for Campus Crusade for Christ in East Asia and national director in Korea, visited their hometown to raise funds for a training center. Tom and Brenda were helping to gather a few people to hear about the opportunity and thought that was the extent of their involvement. However, the Lord burdened them to give personally an amount well beyond their means.

Tom and Brenda had to be creative in funding their commitment. One way was to give all the interest from

their savings for their son's college for a year. This proved
a real sacrifice since they had counted on the interest to
help him through his freshman year.

After they fulfilled their pledge, a friend who knew
nothing of their commitment gave them a cash gift for their
son's college expenses. The amount was more than double
what they had given.

"It is always a privilege when God calls on us to give
above and beyond," says Tom. "It's always exciting to see
how He provides."

A Valuable Lesson

As we faithfully give, God often blesses by teaching us
valuable lessons that far exceed any monetary return.

When Franklin became a Christian, God gave him a
desire to give. At the end of the year, after determining his
gross income, he set aside 10 percent of his earnings for the
work of the Lord.

One year he decided to give his tithe in advance because so many of those to whom he was sending support
needed the funds immediately. In early March, he gave 10
percent of his expected gross income for the year. Then a
truly amazing thing happened.

In his line of business, his income varies considerably. Immediately, it stopped, forcing him to live the rest of
the year on his savings and on funds borrowed against his
assets.

"Through this," Franklin says, "I learned to live well
on considerably less than I had ever thought possible.

"My giving that year, when matched against my income, was almost three times the amount of my usual 10
percent. This taught me that I could give considerably more
than I had ever given. Since that time my giving has ex-

ceeded 10 percent."

And God rewarded Franklin for his faithfulness. Since that year, his business and income have significantly increased.

Franklin tells of another lesson he learned. "We should always live below our income so we can be able to give more. Otherwise, there is no satisfaction from our earnings."

God Honors Faithful Giving

Ever since Margaret and her husband became Christians, they tithed faithfully. Every payday for nearly forty years until his death they gave their tithe first, then they paid their bills.

As a widow, Margaret remains faithful in her giving, encouraged by many memories of how God always met her family's needs through the years. She recalls one Christmas when they had no funds to buy their children presents.

"We never believed in charge accounts or credit cards," she says, "but we would put things on layaway occasionally. This was the case that Christmas. We had gifts laid away for the children, but Christmas was going to come two days before payday. We had given our tithe and paid all our bills, but didn't have enough left to cover the layaway."

How were they going to explain to three little girls why there would be no gifts under their Christmas tree? God in His infinite mercy used a person whom they had never met to supply their need.

"This dear lady sent us a Christmas card, the only one I ever received from her," Margaret recalls. "Enclosed was a $100 check. Well, praise the Lord, we were able to get the gifts out of layaway."

Faith Stretched and Strengthened

While supplying their needs, God used a difficult time financially in the lives of Wesley and Patricia to teach them much about budgeting and His principles of stewardship.

Wesley underwent major back surgery and was unemployed from January 1987 until April 1988. As a self-employed truck driver he received no disability or worker's compensation. The only income they had came from Patricia's small salary and their savings.

Even so, they continued giving to their church and supporting three missionaries. As the couple trusted God to meet their needs, money came from many sources — from the sale of various things, overtime at Patricia's job, a forgotten paid-up insurance policy and anonymous gifts.

"Whenever it looked like we just couldn't make it financially," Patricia says, "the Lord would open up another avenue and provide for us."

On one occasion God provided by helping Patricia find a sizeable error in the family checkbook. As the deadline approached on a bill for $700, Patricia spent the morning in prayer asking God to meet their need. As she prayed, their bank statement arrived in the mail. To her surprise, she discovered that she had neglected to write down a $600 deposit the previous month. That amount plus what she had available brought her account balance up to the amount needed with $75 to spare.

"Thankfully, my husband has returned to work," Patricia says, "but God used that time to stretch and strengthen our faith in Him."

Seeking First the Kingdom

Gordon and Amy are on staff with Athletes in Action. Moving to California from Colorado shortly after their wedding, they faced a difficult adjustment financially. Their rent was double in California what they had paid in Colorado. Other living expenses were higher, too, forcing them to live on a tight budget from paycheck to paycheck.

During their church missions conference, God impressed upon them to increase their missions giving.

"The only problem was that we did not know where to squeeze the money out of our budget," Gordon says. "About that time one of our larger financial supporters had stopped giving to us. We decided to take a large portion of our savings to pay off my school loan. By doing this we freed up $50 a month that we could use to increase our missions giving."

The immediate way in which God affirmed their decision surprised them. Within a month after increasing their giving, the Lord sent them three new supporters. In addition, two checks came in the mail that month from others who had never supported them.

"The way God quickly responded to our financial needs after we obeyed Him in our giving really underscored the principle of stewardship to us," Gordon says. "This reminded us that if we seek first His kingdom and righteousness, God will use His wondrous riches in Christ Jesus to give us everything we need."

Experiencing the Adventure

Would you like to know and experience this joyful adventure of giving by faith?

Preparation for any journey is essential. If you plan to go white water rafting on the Colorado River, for example, you will need to be physically fit. You would have to practice holding your breath for extended periods in case of a mishap. You would need to collect your equipment and pack food and personal items for the trip.

Most importantly, you would select a guide who knows the currents and dangerous rocks, and who can handle emergencies and accidents.

I urge you to equip yourself for your journey in stewardship by prayerfully and carefully following the principles set forth in this book. Make available to God every facet of your time, talent and treasure. I assure you on the authority of God's integrity and the promises of His holy, inspired and inerrant Word that you will enjoy a miraculous and exciting adventure in giving.

For Reflection, Discussion and Action

1. How would you describe your present feelings toward stewardship?

  ☐ Exciting, fulfilling, adventuresome

  ☐ Dread, drudgery, resistant

  ☐ Uniformed, unsure

What would you like your attitude to be by the time you finish this book? Why?

2. Make a list of people you know who give faithfully to God's work. Ask them to share their experiences of joyful giving.

3. Record in a notebook your experiences in giving which produced joy and blessing.

4. Encourage others to give by sharing how God has blessed your giving.

5. Ask the Lord to help you become a godly steward. Record the date and time you begin your adventure in giving by faith.

3

Qualifications of a Steward

Arthur De Moss was a gifted and godly businessman. He built one of the most successful businesses of its kind in America and in the process gained a fortune of an estimated half a billion dollars.

Then suddenly, during an economic recession, stock in his company plummeted. He lost $360 million in only four months—an average of $3 million a day, more than anybody had ever before lost in such a short time. One would think that he would have been devastated, having to cut back on his Christian giving. Instead, he *increased* his giving. As we talked together during that period, Art was rejoicing in the Lord.

"The Lord gave me everything I have," he explained. "It all belongs to Him, and if He wants to take it away that's His business. I don't lose any sleep. I still have a wonderful family and my lifestyle remains unchanged. I will do anything God wants me to do. If He takes away everything He has entrusted to me and calls me to the mission field, I'm ready to go. All He needs to do is tell me."

Art placed his trust completely in his Lord and not in

his fortune. God honored his faith and obedience and eventually restored all that he had lost and much more. Art has now gone to be with the Lord, but his fortune is still being used for the glory of God.

Art's story illustrates an amazingly liberating principle of stewardship. If we faithfully use all that God entrusts to us, and if we keep His ownership of everything in our lives clearly in focus, any material loss simply represents His decision to direct to another the stewardship of that possession. This concept removes the burdensome grief associated with losing what we consider our own, since in fact it is not our own. In times of tragedy, God never forsakes us. He supplies all our needs. As stewards, our task is to trust Him completely.

True Christian Stewardship

A steward, we have seen, oversees the affairs of a household or estate, or manages the accounts and property of another person.

Let's examine now five qualifications of a good steward.

A Good Steward Is Faithful

The apostle Paul wrote, "It is required of stewards that one be found faithful."[1] The Living Bible phrases it this way: "The most important thing about a servant is that he does just what his master tells him to." Faithfulness is dependability — a steady, day-by-day obedience to what God has given us to do.

Every morning when Vonette and I get on our knees before God, we remember that we belong to Him. We acknowledge that we love Him with all our hearts, with all our souls and with all our minds. We ask Him to walk around in our bodies, to think with our minds, to love with our hearts, to speak with our lips. And since He came to seek and to save the lost, we ask Him to continue seeking and saving the lost through us. Throughout the day, we make decisions in light of this commitment.

Obedience to the commands of Scripture, persistence in claiming the promises of God's Word, a daily commitment to "walk in the light as is in the light"[2] and to abide in Christ and let His Word abide in us[3]—these are the qualities of a faithful steward.

A Good Steward Is Trustworthy

As faithfulness relates to dependability, trustworthiness means integrity. If you are honest, your word is your bond. I say to those with whom I work closely, "Please don't ever hesitate to tell me when you have made a mistake. I will understand because we all make mistakes. But never lie to me, never be deceptive or manipulative because inevitably I will learn about it. When I do, I will forgive you, but I will have difficulty trusting you again." I cannot think of any justification for lying or deceitfulness. Because of the untrustworthiness of many Christians, no one can place confidence in them. The most important virtue in life is our integrity. As good stewards, our reputation, our character, our trustworthiness, our integrity must be above reproach.

As a boy, I learned that one's word outweighed any written contract. My grandfather and my father would complete large business deals involving large sums of money with a handshake. They took pride in their integrity. Once my grandfather had several associates who had invested in one of his oil properties. For some reason that project did not develop as he had promised. Although he was not legally obligated, he felt constrained to return their funds. You do not always have control over your wealth, but you are the one who decides whether you can be trusted.

In 1948, while on my way to Oklahoma for a December 30 wedding to Vonette Zachary, I passed through the city of Okmulge where my grandfather had lived for many years. I had visited my grandparents there often. Suddenly, I remembered my need to purchase gifts for the wedding party and stopped at a jewelry store.

Before looking for the items I wanted, I asked the man in charge, whom I later learned was the owner, if he would cash an out-of-state check.

"I'm sorry, sir," he shook his head courteously. "It's against our policy."

I turned to walk out of the store.

"Do you know anyone in this city?" he called after me.

"No. My grandfather used to live here, but he's been dead for several years," I offered.

"What was his name?"

"Sam Bright."

"Are *you* the grandson of Sam Bright?" The man approached with enthusiasm.

I nodded.

"Sam Bright was the most honorable man I have ever known!" he exclaimed. "If you're anything like your grandfather, I will sell you anything in this store. And I'll take your check!"

I felt moved by this experience. Although my grandfather had been gone for many years, he had left a legacy of integrity.

A Good Steward Is Knowledgeable

A good steward must be knowledgeable. In considering investments for our Lord, we must study various Christian enterprises to determine which of them merit our help.

Fund-appeal letters provide a good source of information. "Many Christians get tired of all those letters asking for money that come in the mail," a dear friend told me one day. "But I get excited about them. I'm always looking for a better opportunity to invest my money to serve the Lord. I don't hesitate to say 'no' if the project is a good investment for the kingdom."

I encourage you to seek the counsel of other godly Christians who invest in worthwhile projects. Determine which churches and ministries best fulfill God's plan for your giving and investigate their track records. Ask for financial statements, and enclose with each request a contribution large enough to make the effort worthwhile. Find out how long the ministries have been in existence and what they have accomplished for the cause of Christ. Further, examine the credentials of those who lead the movements.

Common sense, or a "sound mind," is a good guide as well. Paul said to Timothy, "God has not given us a spirit of fear, but of power and of love and of a sound mind."[4] Apply this God-given sense. Invite the Holy Spirit to help you invest your money where you know it will bear the best results for His glory.

A Good Steward Is Fruitful

The measure of good stewardship is fruitfulness. Let us look at a parable that Jesus told to illustrate this point:

> The Kingdom of Heaven can be illustrated by the story of a man going into another country, who called together his servants and loaned them money to invest for him while he was gone.
>
> He gave $5,000 to one, $2,000 to another, and $1,000 to the last—dividing it in proportion to their abilities—and then left on his trip. The man who received the $5,000 began immediately to buy and sell with it and

soon earned another $5,000. The man with $2,000 went right to work, too, and earned another $2,000.

But the man who received the $1,000 dug a hole in the ground and hid the money for safekeeping.

After a long time their master returned from his trip and called them to him to account for his money. The man to whom he had entrusted the $5,000 brought him $10,000.

His master praised him for good work. "You have been faithful in handling this small amount," he told him, "so now I will give you many more responsibilities. Begin the joyous tasks I have assigned to you."

Next came the man who had received the $2,000 with the report, "Sir, you gave me $2,000 to use, and I have doubled it."

"Good work," his master said. "You are a good and faithful servant. You have been faithful over this small amount, so now I will give you much more."

Then the man with the $1,000 came and said, "Sir, I knew you were a hard man, and I was afraid you would rob me of what I earned, so I hid your money in the earth and here it is!"

But the master replied, "Wicked man! Lazy slave! Since you knew I would demand your profit, you should at least have put my money into the bank so I could have some interest. Take the money from this man and give it to the man with the $10,000. For the man who uses well what he is given shall be given more, and he shall have abundance. But from the man who is unfaithful, even what little responsibility he has shall be taken from him."[5]

A faithful steward will scrutinize his opportunities and invest what God has given him in such a way that it will produce the best results.

Even in giving to our church, we should examine its fruitfulness. While studying your church budget, ask yourself these questions: What is my church doing to help fulfill the Great Commission? How many people is it introducing to Christ each year? How many of these are being discipled to grow and mature in their spiritual walk? Does my church show concern for orphans and widows and other needy people?

The master in Jesus' parable held each steward responsible for his investment. He rewarded or rebuked the steward according to his fruitfulness. In like manner, our Lord expects fruitfulness in the "little things" of material wealth before He will entrust us with the true riches of eternal value.[6]

A Good Steward Is Godly

A good steward also lives a godly life. Holiness is God's highest and most glorious attribute. Personal godliness begins with our birth into the family of God. We actually receive into our lives the One who is holy and perfect—the Lord Jesus, the risen Christ. From that moment, Christ begins to develop His life in us, a process which continues throughout our lives.

Some time ago, my heart grieved as I learned of a respected Christian leader who had fallen into a life of sin. He had obviously not intended to do so, but when the temptation came he gave in. As a result his wife, his family, his friends and fellow Christians suffered severe heartache. Most tragically, his testimony and witness for the Lord Jesus has suffered untold damage. Many have ridiculed and rejected the cause of Christ because of his sin.

Since God wants us to live a holy life, the enemy seeks to entrap us in sin and defeat. Several years ago a story in a national magazine described a couple who adopted two wolf cubs, which they discovered while making a film of caribou in Alaska. They took the young wolves to their home and raised them with tender, loving care. For a while the wolves behaved just like friendly dogs. One day, however, they turned on their masters, who barely escaped with their lives. The wolves then fled to join a wild wolf pack. No matter how kindly their masters had treated them, their natures were such that sooner or later they would behave like other wolves.

Similarly, our sinful nature stays the same. No amount of education, refinement, culture, or kindness can take away its selfishness and proneness to sin. Victory is assured only as we live moment by moment under the power and control of the Holy Spirit.

Christians who fall into carnal living do so because they fail to recognize the danger signals in their spiritual walk. The love of self, the love of pleasure, and the love of money consumes and preoccupies them, affecting their giving, their priorities, and their intimacy with God Himself. As a result, Satan robs them of their joy in Christ and destroys their witness as children of God.

How does one live a consistent, godly life? God has given us His Holy Spirit to empower us for holy living and fruitful witness. He releases His power in our lives as we:

- Spend time daily in the presence of God through diligent Bible study and prayer.
- Obey Him in all things and avoid those things that dishonor Him.
- Claim His promises in the face of temptation.
- Keep short accounts with God.

From the beginning of my Christian life, God gave me a strong desire to live a holy life and become a fruitful witness for our Lord Jesus Christ. I really worked at this matter of being a Christian. I attended church several times each week, gave leadership to a witnessing group of more than a hundred young people, and served as a deacon in the church. I studied and memorized Scripture, lived a disciplined life of prayer and witnessed for Christ regularly. Yet, the harder I tried to live the Christian life the more frustrated I became. I often felt guilty and spiritually inadequate.

One day, as I was reading His Word, God graciously showed me how simply one can appropriate the fullness and power of the Holy Spirit to live a godly and fruitful life. He revealed to me the concept I call "Spiritual Breathing," which has enabled me to experience the exciting, wonderful and adventurous joy of walking in the Spirit for more than forty years. Through the years, this concept has enabled millions of Christians around the world to experience God's love and forgiveness in their lives.*

Spiritual Breathing, like physical breathing, is a process of exhaling the impure and inhaling the pure. Think for a moment on how your body needs to breathe. When you exhale, you rid your lungs of carbon dioxide and other impurities that would cause disease if they stayed in your system. Then, when you inhale, you breathe in the oxygen so crucial to maintaining a healthy body.

So it is with spiritual life. Through sin, we break our fellowship with God. As a result, we feel guilty and estranged from our Lord; we become complacent, discouraged and depressed. An exercise in faith, Spiritual Breathing enables us to experience God's love and forgiveness as a way of life.

We "exhale" by confession. Confession means three things; first, we agree with God that whatever we are doing that displeases Him is sin. Next, we acknowledge that

---

* For a more complete discussion of the role of the Holy Spirit in your life, I encourage you to read my book, *The Secret: How to Live With Purpose and Power* (Here's Life Publishers).

Christ has paid the penalty for our sins by shedding His blood and dying on the cross. Then we repent. We experience a change of attitude and action. That is, we turn away from our wrongdoing.

Having confessed our sins, we then "inhale" by appropriating the fullness of God's Spirit by faith. We invite Him to direct, control and empower our life according to His promise in Acts 1:8, "You shall receive power when the Holy Spirit has come upon you."

Spiritual Breathing is the secret to living the Spirit-filled life moment by moment. The Spirit-filled life is one where we surrender the control of the throne of our life to our risen Lord and draw on His power through the enabling of the Holy Spirit to live the Christian life. When we retake control of the throne by a deliberate sin, by worry and anxiety or unbelief, we need to breathe spiritually.

Is sin causing difficulty in your life? Has unconfessed sin begun to accumulate? I encourage you to keep short accounts with God. Whenever you find yourself retaking control of the throne of your life, breathe spiritually. Ask God to give you His power to gain victory over every form of sin, worry, anxiety — whatever you have confessed to Him. You will not only experience a fulfilled, happy life, but you will love our Lord more and thus be more effective as a steward of His blessings.

For Reflection, Discussion and Action

1. Review the five qualifications of a steward. Ask the Holy Spirit to reveal any sin or weakness in your stewardship. Through Spiritual Breathing, confess these barriers to joyful giving.

2. Study the parable found in Matthew 25:14-29 and list the

characteristics you find in the good and bad stewards. Apply these to the way people live today.

3. Up to this point, how have you pictured the godly steward? Has your opinion changed? How will you need to adjust your lifestyle to become a good steward?

4. Do you know a Christian who models the qualifications of a godly steward? What examples in his life point to these qualifications?

5. Think of an example in your life where sin interfered with your giving. How did you handle it? What will you do differently in the future?

4

Attitudes of
a Steward

He gives little who gives much with a frown.
He gives much who gives little with a smile.

One Monday morning a Christian handyman came to work feeling depressed. "What's the matter, George?" his boss asked, noticing his dejection.

George frowned. "Yesterday, I put a quarter in the collection plate," he explained sadly. "That is, I thought I put a quarter in. But when I got home, I discovered that I had put in the five-dollar gold piece you gave me at Christmas."

"Why, George!" his boss exclaimed. "That is no misfortune. After all, that was a good deed and God will reward you for it."

George shook his head slowly. "You can't fool the Lord. He knows that in my heart I wanted to give only twenty-five cents."

The attitude of a steward is vital.

"A good tree does not bear bad fruit, nor does a bad tree bear good fruit," our Lord said. "Every tree is known by its own fruit. For men do not gather figs from thorns, nor do they gather grapes from a bramble bush. A good man out of the good treasure of his heart brings forth good; and an evil man out of the evil treasure of his heart brings forth evil. For out of the abundance of the heart his mouth speaks."[1]

Paul admonishes, "Let everyone give as his heart tells him, neither grudgingly nor under compulsion, for God loves the man whose heart is in his gift."[2]

God's Word characterizes the attitude of a good steward as one of obedience, gratitude and thanksgiving, cheerfulness and joy.

Call to Supernatural Living

Obedience to our heavenly Father is the natural and spiritual outgrowth of our faith. An attitude of obedience softens the soil of our hearts for fruitfulness in every good work, and gives testimony to God's ownership of our possessions.

Our Lord's commands to give are many. "Give to him who asks you, and from him who wants to borrow from you do not turn away,"[3] Jesus said. "Freely you have received, freely give . . . Give to the poor . . . Give alms of such things as you have . . . "[4] In Matthew 25 our Lord tells us to feed the hungry and clothe the needy. He commands us to be hospitable to strangers, visit the sick and minister to those in prison. Sharing with those in need, He teaches, is the same as giving to God.[5]

Through the years I have become increasingly convinced there are no unhappy obedient Christians. Furthermore, I have never met a person who is living a disobedient life who can honestly say that he is happy. I have observed many Christians, however, who have found peace and blessing while going through the most tragic conditions because they were walking with God in faith and obedience.

I recall one wealthy and influential businessman in California who sacrificed everything he had to care for his dying wife. Eventually he spent his fortune seeking to find a cure for her disease.

By the time I learned about their situation, they had lost their expensive home and were living in modest circumstances in a little trailer on a parking lot off one of the main streets in Hollywood. I went to see them with fear and trembling. How in the world could I, a young Christian businessman, identify with this poverty-stricken husband? He had already lost his large fortune and was about to lose his most precious friend and mate of nearly forty years.

The trailer was neat as a pin. When I stepped into their humble home, it was as though I were entering a corner of Heaven. There, sitting beside his dying wife, was this man holding her hand. Both of them had radiant countenances. The joy of the Lord filled the place. I had come to minister to them, but they ministered to me instead. They were trusting God with their lives. Like Job, they were saying, "Though He slay me, yet will I trust in Him."[6]

I will always remember the peace of heart and mind that this couple enjoyed because they had learned to trust and obey the will of God even in the midst of tragedy.

As we obey our Lord, our example will encourage other Christians to abide by God's principles of stewardship. For instance, several years ago I met a young man of modest means who had heard about the Here's Life World strategy to help fulfill the Great Commission. This young man felt impressed to "adopt" the country of Thailand.

We needed about $75,000 for the Here's Life, Thailand campaign. This man proceeded to sell a piece of property for which he received almost that amount. Even though this gift represented most of his savings, he felt impressed of God to pick up the entire cost for that country with the money from the sale.

Many of the volunteers who prepared to reach Bangkok during the Here's Life campaign took the gospel to other cities, villages and hamlets of Thailand. Sometime later I went on a speaking tour of several Asian countries, including Thailand. While there I spoke at the dedication service of 258 Thais who had committed themselves to take the gospel to millions of their countrymen. They were showing the "JESUS" film throughout their country of 48 million people. This all began through the obedient stewardship and sacrificial giving of one American who helped launch Here's Life, Thailand.

God used this story of dedication to inspire several men to give to help fulfill the Great Commission in other countries through Here's Life World. Equally important, the young man's investment had, by 1989, helped to introduce more than 1,300,000 people to Christ, set up more than 18,000 New Life Groups in homes and start 3,338 churches. It is quite probable that apart from his original investment the spiritual harvest now taking place in Thailand would not have been possible.

God has a particular plan for each of us. I cannot suggest to anyone what his lifestyle should be. I do know that God's Word commands us to seek first the kingdom of God and to set our affections on the things above.[7] Whatever God enables us to earn and save during our lifetime He expects us to use as good stewards.

Because of our old nature, we often hold back in our stewardship, fearing we will not have enough for our own needs. But God will not ask of us more than what we have or what He will provide. Nor will He ever ask us to give what is not ours to give.

For your own blessing and benefit, I encourage you to

obey the Lord and pass on this word of admonition to our brothers and sisters in Christ. Many Christians enjoy material success, blessings and benefits without recognizing that God gave them the ability to make and to have wealth. As you model faithfulness in stewardship, you will encourage them to use their God-given resources also for His glory while they can.

If you and I and Christians everywhere will simply obey our Lord's command to lay up treasures in Heaven, we will release vast sums of money to advance His kingdom. As a result, God's people will have the resources to reach hundreds of millions of people for Christ, and fulfill the Great Commission in this generation.

Gratitude and Thanksgiving

An attitude of gratitude and thanksgiving also characterizes a good steward. The apostle Paul admonishes us to "Always be thankful, for this is God's will for you who belong to Christ Jesus."[8]

Thanksgiving shows faith. When we acknowledge our faith in Him through this attitude, even though circumstances suggest there is no hope, God releases His miraculous power and intervention on our behalf. He turns tragedy to triumph, discord to harmony, and defeat to victory.

Many years ago my personal world seemed to be crumbling around me. All that I had worked and planned for in the ministry of Campus Crusade for Christ was hanging by a slender thread. Because of a series of unforeseen circumstances, we were facing a financial crisis that could bankrupt the movement. This would result in the loss of our beautiful facilities at Arrowhead Springs, California.

Many years before I had discovered that when we express faith through thanksgiving, obedience and gratitude to God, He releases His great power on our behalf. He enables us to be more fruitful for Him. So when the word came to me that everything was virtually lost, I fell to my knees and began to praise the Lord.

As I thanked God in the midst of this crisis, His supernatural peace flooded my heart. I felt assured the He would provide the miracle we needed. In a matter of a few days, totally apart from any of my own abilities to solve the problem, God brought the right people into the right circumstances with the funds to save Arrowhead Springs for the ministry.

The Giver God Prizes

Cheerfulness and joy identify the good steward as well. Someone has said, "The Lord loves a cheerful giver, but He will even accept it from a grouch!" A grouch, however, will never experience the joy that comes with giving from a cheerful heart.

The apostle Paul counsels, "Every one must make up his own mind as to how much he should give. Don't force anyone to give more than he really wants to, for cheerful givers are the ones God prizes."[9]

The Greek word translated "cheerful" is *hilaros,* from which we get the word "hilarious." Supernatural, Holy Spirit-directed stewardship is giving with expectation, excitement, joy, praise—even laughter. Indeed, God prizes "hilarious givers" because they are the ones who have discovered that it is truly "more blessed to give than to receive."[10]

Those who give grudgingly or merely from a sense of duty lose the joy of stewardship. They do not realize that giving should be a natural expression of love and obedience to God, who promises to bless them abundantly.

An attitude of hilarious giving comes from our innermost being as a spontaneous response to what God has called us to do.

The story of Norm and Martha Barclay[11] illustrates this principle. When Martha was pregnant with her second child, Norm learned that he was about to lose his job with an aviation firm. They had always given 10 percent of Norm's salary to the Lord's work, and they continued to do so even though they knew the layoff was coming. God faithfully honored their commitment, and only two days after his layoff Norm found a higher-paying job.

A few years later he suffered another layoff—totally unexpected. Because of a recession, the prospects of finding another job seemed bleak.

During this time a guest speaker visited their church, and their Sunday school class took a special offering for him. Norm and Martha decided to give, and many in the class could not believe it. They were amazed that the Barclays were not hoarding every penny, but expecting God to meet their needs. And He did; soon, Norm found a much better job, which enhanced his career.

After their children were grown and gone, Martha went to work for a Christian ministry. With two incomes, the Barclays decided to increase their giving considerably. God blessed them more materially, and they again increased their giving—even when Norm's job at times seemed unstable.

"God continues to supply our needs abundantly," Martha says. "We thoroughly love being able to give hilariously—it's one of the greatest joys we have."

For Reflection, Discussion and Action

1. Make a list of several things God has done for you or given

to you. With gratitude, thank Him for each of them.

2. Honestly consider your attitude. Are you tempted to disobey God in your stewardship? In which way does disobedience seem most troublesome? Ask God to show you how to be faithful in this area.

3. Memorize 1 Thessalonians 5:18 and meditate on it whenever you feel unthankful.

4. Acknowledge the power of God in your life whenever you face trying circumstances. Ask Him to help you live victoriously.

5. Put yourself in the position of the Barclays. How would you have handled the same situation? How will the right attitude change your reactions?

5

Responsibilities of a Steward

Have you paused recently to reflect on the greatness of God, to look upon Him in wonder, or to describe His glory to those around you?

Our responsibility is to know the One who has given us our stewardship. Our primary task in managing all that God entrusts to us is to reflect His character in all that we do and say.

Recently Michael and Elizabeth watched a fireworks display with two of their young nieces. Dozens of adults saw the fireworks, too. The event showed quite a contrast in attitudes.

Adults and children alike stood on the same hill overlooking the city, but an apathetic silence hung over the "grown-ups" as the night sky lit up. However, the children oooooed and ahhhhed loudly at each burst of light. With no inhibition, they shouted the names of the colors exploding in the sky. The children expressed a wonder over the fireworks — they could not fully comprehend, yet they fully appreciated.

How I wish we "grown-ups" would have such child-like enthusiasm when it comes to expressing love for our Lord and excitement over who He is and His marvelous works.

Reflect the Character of God

God's Word reminds us, "the just shall live by faith"[1] and that without faith it is impossible to please Him.[2] The object of our faith is God. One cannot, therefore, live by faith and reflect the character of God without understanding His attributes.

Let me share with you nine attributes of God that will help you begin to understand who He is. This will enable you to more fully trust and obey Him and become a more pleasing and effective steward.

First, *God is sovereign and eternal.* The Scriptures describe Him as the first and the last. He had no beginning. He will have no end. He owes His existence to no one. Above space and time, He provides a permanent foundation and a secure home and resting place for His children.

Second, *God is omnipresent.* Unlimited by space, He is everywhere. His presence fills the heavens and the earth.[3] God is ever with us, to comfort us, to fellowship with us, to give us boldness in telling others about Him.

Third, *God is omnipotent.* He is all-powerful and the provider and sustainer of all things. As the creator, He involves Himself intimately in the affairs of men.

Fourth, *God is omniscient.* He knows everything. His Word teaches us there is no place in the universe to which we can go that will separate us from Him. Nothing escapes His attention or catches Him by surprise.

Fifth, *God is holy.* He alone is completely pure and free from iniquity. Totally committed to goodness, He is at war with evil. Because God's holiness cannot tolerate sin, wrongdoers cannot live in His presence until they have been cleansed by the blood of our Savior and Lord Jesus Christ.

Sixth, *God is love.* He expressed the depth of His love by the cross. God's holiness and moral purity demand punishment for sin. He is long-suffering and patient, however, preferring to give people the opportunity to repent and accept His forgiveness through Christ.

Seventh, *God is truthful.* His truth is the foundation of all knowledge. It does not change or accommodate itself to varying cultures and standards. Truth is essential to God Himself — it has always existed and always will.

Eighth, *God is merciful.* Paul writes, "God is so rich in mercy . . . that even though we were spiritually dead and doomed by our sins, he gave us back our lives again when he raised Christ from the dead."[4]

Ninth, *God is trustworthy.* His truth is inseparable from His character. God cannot mislead or lie, for this would violate His nature. Honesty and integrity are essential to God Himself.

The knowledge of these marvelous characteristics so fills me with the wonder of Him that I am bursting to tell others about His love and forgiveness. I encourage you to study His attributes. Spend time each day in His Word and in prayer, for God has revealed Himself through His Word and in the person of Jesus Christ.

Knowing God and seeking Him more fully enables us to recognize that at any time and in any place He will be our strength in being a faithful steward.

Help Fulfill the Great Commission

A major responsibility of a fruitful steward is to help

fulfill the Great Commission. I am convinced by the examples and teachings of our Lord and the church of the New Testament that every Christian must be an aggressive witness for our Lord.

Christ has given to every Christian the command to "Go into all the world and preach the Good News to everyone, everywhere"[5] and "to make disciples in all the nations."[6] This command, which the church calls the Great Commission, is the duty of every man and woman in every generation who confesses Christ as Lord.

I often recall the statement, "Born to reproduce." God has given to His children a miraculous method called spiritual multiplication for taking the message of His love and forgiveness in Christ to every living person.

The amazing pattern of a strawberry plant beautifully illustrates this concept. Extending from the main vine are several wiry green stems like arms shooting out in different directions. Each of these slender stems reaches across six inches of soil until it penetrates the earth and forms roots of its own. Thus each stem becomes a new strawberry plant.

Until this baby plant sustains itself, it draws life and nourishment from the mother plant via the runner. Once it establishes itself and matures, however, the newborn plant begins to sprout its own runners, replicating itself many more times over.

Spiritual multiplication simply means winning people to Christ, building them in their Christian faith, then sending them out to win and disciple others for our Lord Jesus, generation after generation. Few Christians seem to comprehend that this is the number-one priority in their lives. They become sidetracked with the cares and consequences of materialism and other selfish interests.

The story of two missionary families who settled in the

Oregon Territory in 1836 to evangelize the Cayuse and Nez Perce Indians offers a poignant example.

The Second Great Awakening of the early 19th century and the opening of the West for settlement gave birth to a breed of courageous missionaries who committed themselves to spreading the gospel among the Indians. Led by a spirit of adventure and determination, the Whitmans and Spauldings were typical of these pioneers of the faith.

Heading for Oregon in the spring of 1836, they eagerly looked forward to converting the American Indians. The grueling trip cost them most of their belongings. Once in Oregon the Whitmans settled in Waiilatpu, a lush green valley and home of the Cayuse Indians. The Spauldings located among the Nez Perce at Lapwai, a bleak and dry mountainous area.

At first, neither couple had much time for evangelizing. Far removed from each other, they spent their days building shelters for the coming winter months.

Once settled, the Whitmans and Spauldings began their missions work. In time, however, the Whitmans neglected their calling and became prosperous farmers. The well-cultivated fields of their plantation lay in stark contrast to the humble mission of the Spauldings.

Consumed by the needs of white immigrants, Marcus Whitman sold produce to them as they passed through. His wife, Narcissa, lost the excitement and zeal she initially had for Indian missions and became moody and depressed. Although Marcus worked sacrificially among the Indians as minister and doctor, they resented his prosperity. Even when he tried to help the Cayuse when a plague ravished their villages, they believed he was purposely poisoning them.

Finally, one dreary November afternoon in 1847 the Indians attacked the Whitman plantation and massacred fourteen of the seventy-two people living there. Marcus and Narcissa were among the casualties.

Henry Spaulding, meanwhile, had established a thriving church among the Nez Perce. His wife, Eliza, ran a school for the children and made hand-painted books and translated hymns into their language. Despite opposition to their ministry, they reaped a harvest of souls.

As a result of the massacre, however, American troops ordered all missionaries out of the territory. Henry Spaulding was unable to return to his mission until twenty-four years later. His labors among the Indians bore fruit, soon resulting in revival. A training school was established and eventually the Nez Perce began evangelizing other Indian tribes.

A faithful steward will not stray from his call. Instead, he will invest the resources God has given him wisely and generously for the expansion of the kingdom.

Manage Time, Talent, Treasure

A faithful steward also manages his time, talent and treasure for maximum effectiveness in doing God's will.

Perhaps you have heard the story about the farmer who told his wife he was going out to plow the "south forty." He got off to an early start so he could oil the tractor. He needed more oil, so he went to the shop to get it. On the way he noticed the pigs needed feeding. So he proceeded to the corn crib, where he found some sacks of feed. The sacks reminded him that his potatoes were sprouting. Then when he started for the potato pit, he passed the wood pile and remembered that his wife wanted wood in the house. As he picked up a few sticks, an ailing chicken passed by. He dropped the wood and picked up the chicken. When evening arrived, the frustrated farmer had not even got to the tractor, let alone to the field.

Have you ever intended to do something you knew was important but found yourself distracted by other tasks, which kept you from accomplishing your main goal?

Time is a gift of God, and we must use it wisely. His Word records in Ephesians 5, "Be careful how you walk, not as unwise men, but as wise, making the most of (or redeeming) your time, because the days are evil."[7] God knows what we have to accomplish today.

I like to begin every day on my knees, acknowledging that Jesus Christ is Lord of my life and thus my time. I ask Him to help me evaluate and arrange my priorities.

The stewardship of our talent equally matters. The Holy Spirit has endowed each of us with at least one spiritual gift.[8] We would be poor stewards if we ignored that special ability.

Often people have asked me, "What is the difference between a spiritual gift and natural ability?" The difference is not always clear. All spiritual gifts and natural abilities come from God. Whether our ability stems from a spiritual gift or a natural talent really is not important. God expects us to develop that gift or talent to its fullest potential through the control and empowering of the Holy Spirit. He requires us to exercise much discipline and hard work as we use our talent according to God's will and for His glory.

Matthew 6:21 records perhaps the simplest truth about our commitment to stewardship:

Where your treasure is, there will your heart be also.

One can determine much about a Christian's spiritual life by what he treasures. Our use of money clearly shows our spiritual commitment because where our heart is, our treasure will follow.

Reclaim Souls for Christ

A steward is the guardian of human souls, a concept seldom considered in the context of stewardship.

The only treasure anyone will have in Heaven is what he lays up through his efforts for God here on earth. The greatest treasures of all will be the souls we bring to Jesus Christ through the investment of our time, talent and treasure. Although man has turned away from God, he is still God's creation. God has chosen to use human instruments to bring repentant individuals back to Himself. By bringing an unbeliever into our lives, He grants us the joyful opportunity of stewardship in reclaiming that soul for Him.

Let me share with you several ways in which we can be faithful stewards of souls.

First, *pray for the lost.* Think of someone you know who needs Christ, and pray specifically for that person. Ask the Holy Spirit to send someone across your path who needs to hear the message of God's love and forgiveness. Pray for the power and boldness you will need to speak to that individual. .

Second, *trust the Holy Spirit* to open the understanding of that person's mind and to prepare his heart. Whenever I am with a person for even a few minutes, I consider that a divine appointment. I believe God has brought us together because that person needs to hear the gospel.

Being a steward of souls is like being a good businessman. He always has his antenna out for anything that looks like a better investment for his dollar. If I neglect a divine appointment, I am not a good steward of that opportunity. A good steward of souls will get up in the morning and say, "Now, Lord, who do you want me to talk to today?" All day long—on the plane, in the office, or out on the campus—he is ever sensitive to the leading of the Holy

Spirit.

Third, *draw on the power of the Holy Spirit to enable you to tell the individual about Christ.* Share your faith with him, confident that the Holy Spirit is helping you. If you have never received training in how to tell others about Christ, let me suggest you read *Witnessing Without Fear: How to Share Your Faith With Confidence* (Here's Life Publishers). In this book, I have shared a proven, step-by-step approach that will help you witness effectively for our Lord.

Fourth, *leave the results to God.* Many will listen to the gospel and gladly receive the Lord. Others will reject Him. But don't get discouraged. Even Jesus was unable to bring everyone to whom He spoke into His kingdom. Our task is simply to take the initiative to share. God must change the person's heart.

We have all heard the popular expression, "You can't take it with you." When Howard Hughes died, someone asked, "How much money did he leave?" Another replied, "All of it." True, we cannot take our material possessions with us. For all eternity we will enjoy riches that we do not deserve. The one thing we will not have in Heaven is the priceless privilege of introducing souls to our Savior. As fruitful Christian stewards here on earth, however, we will take with us to heaven every soul we have brought to Christ.

For Reflection, Discussion and Action

1. Remind yourself of the greatness of God by praising Him for His creative wonders.

2. Review the attributes of God listed in this chapter. Study these attributes in depth, using the concordance in your

Bible and other helps.

3. Make a list of people around you who do not know the Lord Jesus as their Savior and pray for them. Using the four steps listed in the chapter, take the initiative to share your faith with them as the Lord leads.

4. Begin every day this week by acknowledging Jesus as the Lord of your life. Ask the Holy Spirit to help you prioritize your time, talent and treasures.

5. Memorize Matthew 6:21. Evaluate your checkbook to see where your treasure lies.

Part 2

Keys to God's Abundant Blessings

6

The Principles
of Giving

"Go break to the needy sweet charity's bread; For giving is living," the angel said.

"And must I be giving again and again?" My peevish and pitiless answer ran.

"Oh no," said the angel, piercing me through.

"Just give till the Master stops giving to you!"[1]

During a speaking engagement at Wheaton College, a senior named Jim Green approached me. "I don't know what God wants me to do with my life," he sighed. "I need to talk to you."

A gifted person, Jim could have pursued a career in several fields. I shared with him briefly how he could discover God's will for his life according to Scripture, then hurried off to another appointment.

When Jim approached me later that afternoon, he was excited. "The biblical formula you gave me works! Not only has God revealed what He wants me to do, but He has shown me the organization He wants me to be associated with!"

Nearly thirty years have passed since we talked and prayed together. Jim has served on our staff for twenty-six years, thirteen of which have been as a missionary in remote areas of Africa. He and his precious wife, Nan, are truly two of the Lord's greatest servants whom I know. They constantly seek to strengthen the arms of the national leadership.

Yesterday, as we were talking about the need for funds for a particular work in Africa, I felt that we as an organization should seek to raise the money for the project. However, Jim volunteered to provide for the ministry out of his and Nan's personal income.

"We have discovered that the more we give to God, the more He blesses us," he enthused.

As missionaries, Jim and Nan are already pouring out their hearts for materially needy and spiritually hungry people. One would hardly expect them to give more, but they have learned to take God at His word and give generously by faith, trusting Him to provide for their personal needs to enable them to help meet the needs of others.

Many years ago Dr. Oswald Smith, the famous Canadian evangelist and missionary statesman, spoke on stewardship to his congregation. "You can't beat God at giving," he said. "If you will deal honorably with God in money matters, obeying the command to 'Bring all the tithes into the storehouse,' God will prosper you spiritually and materially."

Among his listeners was a man who had lost his job and was suffering severe financial difficulty. Challenged by Dr. Smith's message, he decided to give God's work a tenth of his future earnings.

To his great joy, the man found employment within a short time. As he worked diligently and remained faithful to his commitment, he advanced steadily in his job and received increases in salary with each promotion.

"I owe much to you for your challenging message on tithing," he later testified to Dr. Smith. "I have proven God's faithfulness to do exactly what He says."

Why Is Giving Necessary?

Why is it so important to give? Because God's Word says so!

The Bible records more than seven hundred references to giving. The New Testament has more to say about this subject than about the return of Christ.

Let me share with you eight basic reasons for giving.

First, *giving began with God.* His supernatural expression of giving was in the sacrifice of His only begotten Son that we might receive forgiveness for our sins, become children of God, and enjoy eternal life. God continues to give of Himself today in love, forgiveness, peace, purpose and power. By this He enables us to live full, meaningful lives. The source of all life, He continues among other things to provide us with food, air, water, shelter and clothing.

Second, *giving is a law of God.* After the Flood, God made a covenant that "While the earth remains, seedtime and harvest . . . shall not cease."[2] From the beginning, the law of the harvest has governed nature and formed the means for God's abundant blessings. When our Lord said, "Give and it will be given you," He was referring this principle. Giving is not optional for the believer. Jesus commanded us to "Give to him who asks you, and from him who wants to borrow from you do not turn away."[3] He said, "Freely you have received, freely give."[4]

Third, *giving was the lifestyle of our Lord.* A concise

description of His lifestyle appears in the Book of Acts, which records, "He went about doing good."[5] Jesus gave in feeding the multitudes. He gave in healing the sick. He gave in teaching His disciples. He gave in empowering His disciples for evangelism. He gave in compassion for the poor. He gave in offering rest to the weary. He gave in dying on the cross for our sins. He gave in sending His Holy Spirit.

Our Lord spoke about giving as much as, if not more than, any other subject. Half of His recorded parables concern our stewardship of money, property, time, skills and relationships with others in dealing with material possessions. He taught us that the secret to abundance is to "Give, and it will be given to you, good measure, pressed down, shaken together, and running over will be put into your bosom."[6]

Fourth, *giving is the essence of being.* I have often shared the story of a baby girl who lay near death, critically injured in an automobile accident. She desperately needed a blood transfusion, but doctors could find no one who had her rare blood type. In the midst of their frantic search, the doctors discovered that the child's older brother, Kevin, had the right type. Anxious to proceed, one of the doctors sat down with the seven-year-old boy and talked quietly with him.

"Your sister is very sick, son," he said somberly. "If we don't help her, she's not going to live. I want to know if you are willing to give your blood to help your baby sister?"

His face pale with fear, Kevin seemed to struggle with his answer. Then, after a few moments, he said softly, "Yes, I will."

The little boy watched sadly and silently as his blood flowed from his arm through the tube.

"We're almost finished," the doctor smiled encouragingly.

Kevin's eyes filled with tears. "How long till I die?" he whispered.

Looking at him in amazement, the doctor realized that Kevin thought he was to give all his blood to save his sister. That brave little boy had believed that his act of mercy would cost him his life, yet he was willing to do it!

I wonder, how far are we willing to go in helping others? How much of ourselves are we willing to give?

Fifth, *giving is the basis of receiving.* There is a vast difference between giving *to* receive and receiving *because* we give. We cannot manipulate or bribe God. In giving we cannot say, "Ten will get me a hundred," or — to put it crudely — "God, my pocket is flat, so here's a buck to make it fat." He will not honor such an attitude.

Giving is the basis of receiving because it is a law of God. Only what we give to God can He multiply back to us in the form of supply.[7] Multiplication is the mathematics of Heaven. God commanded Adam and Eve to "be fruitful and multiply."[8] In His covenant with Abraham, God promised, "I will multiply your descendants as the stars of the heaven and as the sand which is on the seashore."[9] The apostle Paul records that God can "supply and multiply the seed you have sown."[10] On two occasions our Lord multiplied a few loaves and fishes to feed the multitudes who followed Him.[11] Whatever we give becomes the basis of God's multiplication because He applies to giving the law of sowing and reaping.[12]

Sixth, *giving brings blessing.* Money symbolizes our skill and effort in life. When we give of our possessions, we are essentially giving of ourselves. In the process we become channels of blessing.

The Sea of Galilee provides a good example of this. Because it receives and passes on its fresh, sweet water, the sea is a source of life. The surrounding plains are among the most fertile in the world.

A harp-shaped lake in the Jordan valley, the Sea of Galilee is fed by the Jordan River, which exits through a broad fertile valley at the southern tip of the lake. The region produces abundant crops of wheat, barley, fruit and vegetables. Wild flowers and oleanders fringe the shoreline. The region was an important center of New Testament events, and Christ performed a third of His recorded miracles there.[13]

By contrast, the Dead Sea — just sixty-five miles down stream — is a harsh, saline body of water. Like the Sea of Galilee, its fresh water source is the Jordan. Unlike the Sea of Galilee, however, the Dead Sea has no outlet. As a result, the water is bitter to taste and nauseous to smell.

The sea is so salty and so saturated with minerals that one can literally lie on his back and read a newspaper. I did this once when I was visiting there. The surrounding area is a barren chaos of crags and wadis where even the Bedouin flocks find little sustenance, reinforcing the effect of life-less shores around a lifeless sea. This intensely salty lake would be fresh or only mildly saline if it had an outlet.

Two bodies of water — one sweet and overflowing with blessing; the other, bitter and lifeless. One receives and gives, the other receives and hoards.

Traveling the world, I have observed many Christians who can be typified by these waters. Like the Sea of Galilee, some are refreshed by "rivers of living water."[14] They give abundantly to the work of our Lord with enthusiasm and excitement. They are prosperous and filled with joy, "abounding in the work of the Lord."[15]

I also have seen those who hang onto what God has entrusted to them, trying to build larger and larger estates. These people are usually cantankerous, negative, unhappy and anti-social. What joy they have missed because, like the

Dead Sea, their channel became blocked by greed and selfishness!

Seventh, *giving ministers to the Lord Jesus.* When we perform loving acts for others, our Lord records each kindness as if we had done it for Him personally. Our heavenly Father considers the smallest gesture—even a cup of cold water given to a thirsty person in His name—to be a gift from us to His beloved Son.

Eighth, *giving removes stumbling blocks to faith.* In presenting the gospel of our Lord Jesus Christ to others, sometimes we meet those who are hungry, out of work, sick or burdened with other problems. What should be our response to their needs? Share Christ and be on our way? It is difficult—if not impossible—for them to listen to our witness until we translate our faith in Christ into loving care for their necessities. The apostle James says:

> What does it profit, my brethren, if someone says he has faith but does not have works? If a brother or sister is naked and destitute of daily food, and one of you says to them, "Depart in peace, be warmed and filled," but you do not give them the things which are needed for the body, what does it profit? . . . I will show you my faith by my works.[16]

As we meet the special needs of those in distress, their hearts will be more open to receive God's love and forgiveness. This would enable us to do the most valuable work of all—introducing them to our wonderful Savior.

Giving Is for Everyone

The law of Spirit-directed giving applies to everyone. From earliest youth to oldest age, rich or poor, we are all commanded of God to give.

Love for God and obedience to His will is the criteria for giving. God desires to bless His children abundantly and promises to do so, if only we will demonstrate faith in Him through trust and obedience to Him. Are you having difficulty meeting your financial obligations and providing food for your family? One of the best things you can do is find someone who has greater needs than yourself and share out of your meager resources. In the process, Paul says, "God is able to make it up to you by giving you everything you need and more, so that there will not only be enough for your own needs, but plenty left over to give joyfully to others."[17]

It Is More Blessed to Give

The Book of Acts records the words of the Lord Jesus, "It is more blessed to give than to receive."[18]

I remember I first heard this as a growing lad, then as an agnostic and later as a young Christian. I could not comprehend how giving could be better than receiving. Now that I have been a Christian for many years, I truly understand. It is "more blessed to give" than to receive for several reasons.

First, *God created us within the context of a giving universe.* When one chooses to contradict God's design, he suffers the consequences: greed, competitiveness, gross shortages, imbalances of wealth distribution and insecurity.

Second, *giving is more productive.* When we give freely of ourselves and of our possessions as a material expression of our spiritual obedience to Christ, God in turn meets our needs in abundance.

The story of a Christian newspaper reporter whose family was experiencing a severe financial need illustrates this point. During an appeal for a special project at their church, the reporter felt impressed to give. Uncertain about the amount, he prayed, "Lord, how much should I give?"

The reply flashed into his mind as clearly as though it were spoken aloud. "You may give anything between ten and twenty-five dollars."

Reaching for his check book, he scrawled $20 on a check and dropped it into the offering bag as it passed. A deep sense of peace settled over him as he began to trust God to supply his own need.

A short time later, the reporter and his wife put their house up for sale. The real estate agent shook his head as he wrote up the listing. "You'll never sell it at that price," he warned.

In less than two weeks, however, the couple had two buyers — each at full price. "By the time our negotiations ended," they testified, "we had a guaranteed sale at two thousand dollars above market value. Then we realized what God had done. He had multiplied our twenty dollars a hundred fold."

Meanwhile, the reporter had felt led to give another Christian ministry a gift of thirteen dollars. Again, trusting God to supply his own need, he wrote out a check for the amount and dropped it in the mail. In the weeks to come, God miraculously enabled him to save thirteen hundred dollars on the purchase of another home.

Third, *giving begins an endless circle of joy.* God gives; we receive. We give; He receives. He then multiplies what we have given back to us in the form of our supply.

Throughout Scripture, we find that whenever a command to give appears, God also gives a promise of return.[19] If we are giving to glorify God, we can expect a return that is more than the gift. The purpose of the return is that we may have the ability to give again, thus completing the circle.

Giving by Faith

Giving by faith is a principle basic to Spirit-directed stewardship. Simply defined, giving by faith is taking God at His Word and giving generously as He provides.

The premise of this concept is three-fold. First, God is the absolute source of our supply. Second, giving is based on His resources, not our own. Third, Christ is our link to God's inexhaustible riches. The apostle Paul includes these precepts in his letter to the Christians at Philippi:

> My *God shall supply* all your need *according to his riches* in glory *by Christ Jesus.*[20]

Let's look at each for a moment.

God shall supply. Living in a humanistic society, it is easy to believe that man is our source of wealth. When in need, we look to people and to institutions for help. Indeed, God uses them in His process of provision, but they are the instruments — not the source — of our supply.

In placing our trust in people or things, it does not take long to discover their limitation in helping us. Acknowledging God as the total source of all that we need gives us a clear vision of His greatness and power to provide.

According to His riches. Our heavenly Father holds the treasures of Heaven and earth in His hands. His supply is not based on the size of our need, but on the enormity of His riches. In good times and bad, His reserve remains stable and inexhaustible.

As God's stewards, we have opportunity to reflect His bountiful wealth. At times God will impress us to give what we cannot give. Then we must call upon His "riches in glory" rather than depend on our limited reservoir.

By Christ Jesus. We appropriate God's abundant blessings through Christ. The apostle Paul records, "though he was so very rich, yet to help you he became so very poor, so that by being poor he might make you rich."[21] Our Lord laid aside His riches in Heaven to identify with us in every area of our human need. When He returned to His Father, God reinvested Him with all that He had laid aside—His infinite power, His unspeakable glory, and His inexhaustible riches.

As children of God, we identify with the death, burial and resurrection of our Lord. By miraculous intervention, God placed us in Christ. When Jesus died on the cross, we died. When He arose from the grave, we arose. When He ascended into Heaven, we ascended. Now, we sit with Him in the heavenly realms as joint-heirs with Christ, blessed with "every spiritual blessing in the heavenly places in Christ."[22]

The moment we accepted Christ as our Savior and Lord, we received this inheritance.[23] Because of our Lord's glorified position in Heaven, and since He is with us now through His Holy Spirit, we have all sufficiency in Him.

Give With a Sense of Urgency

If we ever plan to do anything for Christ and His kingdom, we must do it now. Growing worldwide problems and unprecedented opportunities for Christian ministry make giving an urgent priority.

This morning I spoke with a businessman who is involved in a $120 million property transaction. This project potentially would enable him to make tens of millions of dollars in profit.

"I must act right away!" he exclaimed. "If I don't close the deal immediately, I'll lose it."

This man spoke of a business transaction with all the danger of a hasty decision. How much more, when we think about the eternal destiny of billions of people, should we be constrained and motivated by a sense of urgency!

Every Christian is responsible to help reach his own generation for Jesus Christ. We cannot be casual or indifferent about our task. We would make every effort to rescue a drowning person; let us place the same importance upon our time, talents and treasure in taking the message of Christ to everyone who will listen.[24]

For Reflection, Discussion and Action

1. Are you preoccupied with things? How have they affected your giving? What steps can you take to avoid this entanglement in the future?

2. List several examples of how Jesus gave to others. Discuss how you could follow His lead by doing similar actions.

3. Think of an instance in your life that illustrates each of the three reasons why giving is better than receiving.

4. Memorize Philippians 4:19, taking note of the three-fold premise of giving out of God's resources outlined in the chapter. Remind yourself of this verse each time your faith to give is tested.

7

The Basis
of Giving

Every year, America's hard-working farmers harvest billions of bushels of barley, corn, oats, wheat and rye. They reap in the fall what they sowed in the spring. Assuming proper soil and weather conditions, they reap bountifully— many times more than what they planted.

The provision of God is based on the law of the harvest: *What we sow we will reap.* This law is as inviolate as the law of gravity. As sure as the sun will rise and set tomorrow, one can be certain, "Whatever a man sows, that he will also reap."[1]

The law of the harvest is governed by five basic principles of sowing. Ignoring these axioms, when applied spiritually, can devastate our life and witness. By obeying them, however, we can experience life in all of its fullness as our Lord intended.

The First Principle of Sowing

Everything begins with a seed. Whatever we give will return to us because what we give is a seed we sow.

God established this precept long ago. On the third day of creation He commanded, "Let the earth burst forth with every sort of grass and seed-bearing plant, and fruit trees with seeds inside the fruit, so that these seeds will produce the kinds of plants and fruits they come from."[2] Like begets like. To grow vegetables, we must plant vegetable seeds. To produce wheat, we must plant kernels of wheat. To reap anything, we must first plant a seed. Certainly we cannot underestimate the incredible ability of even the smallest kernel.

Perhaps you have seen a tiny seedling pushing and prodding its way through a crack in your sidewalk. I am amazed at the energy that a sprout must exert to bore its way through arid, packed soil or hardened asphalt. I marvel as each spring a mass resurrection of seeds bursts into green carpets of grass, decorating even the crevices in the rocky hillsides surrounding our offices at Arrowhead Springs.

It is not surprising that our Lord placed such importance in the power of a seed, for within it lies the mighty forces of life and growth.

This principle applies spiritually as well as physically. The apostle Paul said, "Whatever a man sows, that he will also reap. He who sows to his flesh will of the flesh reap corruption, but he who sows to the Spirit will of the Spirit reap everlasting life."[3]

Jesus likened faith to a seed planted for a result. With faith even as small as the mustard seed, Jesus said, ". . . nothing will be impossible for you."[4]

Why are these analogies significant? The seed contains the miraculous components of creation.

The Second Principle of Sowing

To reap a bountiful harvest we must sow our best seed.

A few years ago, Daryl was reading a passage from the Book of Leviticus while eating breakfast in a restaurant.

> Whoever offers a sacrifice of peace offering to the Lord, to fulfill his vow, or a freewill offering from the cattle or the sheep, *it must be perfect to be accepted;* there shall be no defect in it.[5]

While studying this passage, he wondered, *Why does God demand perfection? Why should we give Him the best?*

As Daryl meditated upon this thought, the principle became clear. *Theologically,* he mused, *God demanded a perfect sacrifice because it prefigured the Perfect Sacrifice to come—the Lamb of God who would take away the sins of the world. An imperfect offering would have corrupted the symbol of redemption.*

Another principle also is involved. God demands our finest because He uses what we give as the basis of His supply. There is no second best with God. His provision is perpetually perfect and always abundant. Since He cannot give us second best, we frustrate the grace of God and incur His displeasure when we do not give Him our best.

Farmers know this principle well. The story is told of a midwestern wheat farmer who faithfully supplied his neighbors with all the seed they needed to plant. Each year he would give them his choice seed and refuse to accept payment, insisting that they plant only what he supplied. After several years, the farmers finally learned why.

"I give you my best seed every year because I know that what you plant will affect my harvest. My farm is between the rolling hills on which your wheat grows. When our grain begins to grow, pollination occurs. If you don't plant the highest quality of grain, my quality of return is also affected. I give my best so I can harvest the best."

Every Christian should seek to maximize his time, talents and treasure with training and good counsel to produce the greatest spiritual harvest. Many Christians are unhappy and miserable as stewards because they do not give God their best, first, in obedience to the law of the harvest. The best of our lives—the best of our time, the best of our talent, the best of our treasure, the best of everything we have—should be on the altar of sacrifice to God.

The Third Principle of Sowing

An abundant harvest springs from the most fertile soil.

No intelligent farmer would think of planting inferior seed in poorly prepared soil using worn-out equipment. Rather, he would buy the choice seed and prepare the soil thoroughly with the finest equipment and fertilizers available.

The quality of the ground and its preparation are vital. Ideally, the soil must be heavy enough not to be easily eroded by the wind, yet light enough to mix well when tilled.

Good earth holds the moisture and allows the roots to penetrate the ground. Hard soil won't allow water to soak in and eventually becomes unproductive. Sand dries out too quickly. Black, rich dirt that contains no alkali, clay or sand is most suited for holding moisture, because it does not dry out as fast under hot, windy conditions.

Cultivation is crucial as well. The soil must be tilled until soft enough for planting, but not so loose that it will dry out. Tilling also rids the soil of weeds, which rob moisture from the seedlings and prevent the sunlight from producing strong, healthy plants.

The soil in which our financial giving develops also is vital. I marvel at the lifestyle of the average Christian, which differs little from that of nonbelievers in attitudes, actions, motives, desires and words. All of this concerns the

type of soil in which we plant our seed. Many Christians —
even those who give faithfully — experience financial
problems, emotional turmoil, even physical illness, because
they are sowing poor seed in the unproductive soil of wrongful motives and unworthy enterprises.

Like planting good seed in fertile ground, our task as
stewards is to sow righteously. "Sow with a view to
righteousness, reap in accordance with kindness," admonished Hosea.[6]

We cannot appraise good stewardship by the amount
of our gifts, but by how well we put them to good use.
Rooted in fertile soil, righteous giving measures the
stewardship of any gift by how well it reflects the will of
God. Giving for the sake of giving, or contributing where
our gifts are likely to be used for unrighteous purposes, is
not only poor stewardship, but contrary to the will of God.
In the parable of the talents,[7] the nobleman did not fault
the unrighteous steward because he failed to maximize the
return on his investment. Rather, he denounced the
steward because he did not properly use his money.[8]

Righteous stewardship is a function of knowledge.
Wherever we give, we must determine whether our gift will
be used for the glory of God. Our local church, a well-known
Christian ministry, or a popular charity do not necessarily
qualify automatically. Since our Lord came to seek and to
save the lost and He has commissioned us to do the same,
the most fertile ground for giving is the soil that produces
a harvest of fruitful disciples to help fulfill the Great Commission.

The Fourth Principle of Sowing

If we sow our best seed in the most fertile soil, we can
expect an abundant return.

The axiom of abundant return is simple: The crop is

always abundantly more than its seed.

A single redwood tree can reproduce itself millions of times during its lifetime. A lone grape seedling is capable of branching into a prolific vine filled with luscious fruit. One peach pit will sprout into a huge tree laden with its delicious produce.

A wheat, barley, flax and sunflower farmer in North Dakota, Dennis plants a given amount of seed each season for a desired yield per acre. From one-and-a-half bushels of wheat, he expects to harvest up to forty bushels. Under favorable growing conditions, about two bushels of barley will bear roughly seventy bushels. A two-thirds bushel of flax will produce about twenty bushels, and one-eighth bushel or four pounds of sunflower seed will return up to 1,500 pounds.

I believe that if every Christian understood the law of sowing and reaping, the Christian world would experience a dramatic, revolutionary change.

I have the privilege of working with hundreds of dedicated laymen who have discovered the law of abundant return. Again and again they have seen the truth of God's promise — the more they have sown, the more they have reaped.

One often hears the expressions, "You can't outgive God" and "I gave by the spoonful, but God returned to me by the shovelful." God will never be in our debt. He designed the crop to be more than the seed. As we sow obediently and joyfully in faith and righteousness to our Lord, we can expect His abundant return.

The Fifth Principle of Sowing

To bear fruit, however, a seed must die.

Nearing the destined hour of His crucifixion, our Lord

spoke of death as the gateway to life. "Unless a grain of wheat falls into the ground and dies, it remains alone," He said. "But if it dies, it produces much grain."[9]

Planted in the ground, a kernel of wheat goes through an amazing metamorphosis. Dying in the process, it loses its own identity and gives up its previous existence. Life cannot spring from a dead seed, however. A change must take place. The seed must germinate to produce its seedling. The rain comes, and the hard, outer shell begins to soften under the pressure. The secret life buried inside the kernel begins to swell and eventually splits the shell and cracks it open. Only by this dissolution can the seed sprout and send forth abundant fruit. Thus life rises out of apparent death to produce its abundant harvest.

Using this metaphor to explain His own death, our Savior envisioned Himself the seed of righteousness. Apart from the cross, He would be like a single unplanted kernel—inactive and unfruitful. His death and resurrection, on the other hand, would produce many new kernels for an abundant harvest of new lives. His disciples could not grasp the paradox. Unable to see beyond the humiliation of His crucifixion and the sorrow and separation that they would soon experience, death to them meant defeat. But for Jesus, this was not so. Death was His passage to glory and the portal to life for all who would follow Him.

This principle also applies to stewardship. Our Lord said, "He who loves his life will lose it, and he who hates his life in this world will keep it for eternal life."[10] This love-hate paradox teaches that we must be so committed to Christ and controlled and empowered by His Holy Spirit that we die to self. Any love outside this commitment is idolatrous and marked for failure.

Anything in life can become an idol. Money, car, boat, TV, home, hobby, career, ministry, social calendar, friends, family—the list is endless. When possessed with worldly desires and ungodly ambitions, they supplant our love for the Lord. To be fruitful stewards we must die to the selfish attitudes that create these idols.

New attitudes will rise out of the death of our selfishness. Through Spiritual Breathing, the hard shell of our self-centeredness will soften and dissolve, enabling the Holy Spirit to create within us a renewed love for our Lord. This love will produce a bountiful harvest of godly motives, fruitful goals and Spirit-directed priorities.

For Reflection, Discussion and Action

1. Are you giving God your best in stewardship? List ways in which you could improve.

2. Seek a good Christian financial counselor or stewardship training program. Learn how to maximize your giving.

3. Does your lifestyle allow you to develop godly stewardship? Are you experiencing difficulties in your life due to unrighteous attitudes, actions or desires? Prayerfully ask the Holy Spirit to reveal and help you change anything unpleasing to Him.

4. How have you been giving your time, talent and treasure to help fulfill the Great Commission? How do your gifts reflect a desire to see others accept God's love and forgiveness?

5. Describe how each of the five principles of sowing apply to giving by using a practical example for each of them.

8

The Goal of Giving

The story is told of a lighthouse keeper who worked on a treacherous stretch of rocky coastline many years ago. He took immaculate care of the huge lamp that warned the ships. Once a month, he replenished his supply of oil to keep the lamp burning.

The lighthouse keeper enjoyed his work, especially since he was not far from shore and had many guests drop in for visits. Having plenty of time to talk, he got to know the people in the local village well.

One cold night, a widow who had several small children begged him to give her a little oil so she could keep her family warm. Touched by her desperate plea, he poured out a small amount into her jar.

Another night, a father brought his children to visit the lighthouse keeper. Preparing to leave, the father realized that he needed more oil for his lantern so he and his children could find their way back home. Later, someone else needed some oil to lubricate a wheel to avoid an accident. A compassionate man, the lighthouse keeper granted each legitimate request.

Toward the end of the month, his supply of oil ran dangerously low. Since he had never given out any large quantity to any one person, he was surprised. He tried to conserve what he had left, but soon it was gone and his beacon light went out. That very night, several ships were wrecked and many people drowned in the choppy waters.

Authorities investigated the incident and questioned the lighthouse keeper. Although he was repentant and sobbed in remorse, they were unsympathetic. "You were given oil for one purpose only — to keep that light burning! There is no excuse."

As keepers of God's resources, we have but one purpose also — to glorify Him. It is easy to let the day-to-day demands on our finances turn our eyes from this aim unless we clearly define our priorities. God's holy Word does this for us. The biblical order is God, our family, the church, and society.

Priority One: God

Our top priority is to love and obey God. Our Lord said, "You shall love your God with all your heart, with all your soul, and with all your mind. This is the first and great commandment. And the second is like it: you shall love your neighbor as yourself. On these two commandments hang all the Law and the Prophets."[1]

Putting God and the fulfillment of our Lord's Great Commission first in our time, talents and treasure must be the goal of our stewardship. Once this is so, all else falls into place.

Priority Two: the Family

Under God, our family is number one. Since it was the first institution formed by our Creator,[2] no conflict exists between the preeminence of God and the priority of family. Rather, meeting the needs of our family is a scriptural mandate and an evidence of faith.

The apostle Paul admonishes, "If anyone does not provide for his own, and especially for those of his household, he has denied the faith, and is worse than an unbeliever."[3] An individual who neglects his family's needs to give much to many organizations and causes is a poor testimony to the love and care that our heavenly Father has for His children. This principle applies equally to the stewardship of one's time and the sharing of one's companionship.

Within the hierarchy of the family, the needs of the spouse come first, followed by those of the children, the extended family and, finally, one's self.

The spouse. As a husband I am responsible to love Vonette as Christ loved the church,[4] and that is a big commitment. Loving the Lord Jesus with all my heart, soul, mind and strength—my absolute highest objective—enhances my love for her. Often I must work eighteen to twenty hours a day. In the early years of this ministry, my schedule kept me away from home much of the time while Vonette cared for our sons. Now that Zachary and Brad are grown and both are serving the Lord, Vonette and I usually travel together. In all these years, I have never lost sight of her as my first priority. I try to let her know how important she is to me by the little niceties I do for her, and by telling her often how very much I love her. When we are together, I try to be patient, loving, compassionate and sensitive to her needs and not judgmental or critical. I do not take our relationship for granted, but try to show my love for her in tangible and practical ways.

The children. Giving priority to the needs of our spouse does not mean we can neglect our children. They are a gift from God,[5] and He expects us to love them and care for their needs. The psalmist records, "Just as a father has compassion on his children, so the Lord has compassion on those who fear Him."[6] As parents, we model the loving care of our heavenly Father by the way we provide for our children.

Provision goes beyond their financial needs, of course. Children need a caring, touching atmosphere in which parents prove their love. Although spending time with our children is essential, it is how we treat them when we are together that counts. Parents who are patient, loving, understanding and sensitive to their children's needs show them how important they are.

The extended family. The responsibility for the family goes beyond the immediate members to include the extended family — mother, father and grandparents. Unfortunately, many Christians give generously of their time, abilities, and finances to their churches or businesses while their extended families live on the edge of poverty and starve from lack of attention, love and care. God requires us to take care of our own and not to rely on the government, which has neither the understanding nor the resources to provide adequately.

One's self. Personal care also is vital. To give more effectively to others, we must refresh ourselves spiritually and physically. If we are good stewards of our health and appearance, we will be more effective in our Christian witness.

Attention to our own needs does not mean "looking out for number one." I have never met a greedy person who is happy. Truly happy people care for the needs of others, trusting God to provide for their own necessities. Personally, I live modestly and do not see the need to accumulate a lot of things. As a faithful steward, I must wear the cloak of materialism loosely. My possessions do not own me. I control them and determine how to use them to accomplish the most for the glory of God.

Priority Three: the Church

For more than forty years, I have been committed to the church. I became a Christian through the influence of the First Presbyterian Church of Hollywood, where I was also nourished in my faith as a young believer.

Shortly after receiving Christ, I began graduate study at Princeton Theological Seminary and later transferred to Fuller Theological Seminary. I continued my studies for five years while also directing my business interests in Los Angeles and serving as a deacon and chairman of evangelism in the church. In 1951 God gave Vonette and me the vision for Campus Crusade for Christ. From the beginning we viewed ourselves as an evangelistic arm of the church, and we have always encouraged our staff to involve themselves actively in local congregations. So we view the church that is obedient to our Lord's command as the most vital part of the work that God is doing in the world.

Our stewardship to the church provides a support base for local evangelism, the church staff, and world missions.

Local evangelism. The church that faithfully exalts our Lord and proclaims His holy, inspired Word is God's primary institution for worship and outreach to a spiritually needy world. As stewards of God's resources, we must help advance the cause of Christ through His local body. We must give whatever we can to edify the church, whether through our tithes and offerings or by teaching Sunday school, serving on various committees, participating in the evangelism and visitation programs, or washing windows on church work day.

By giving to the needs of the church — the mortgage, utilities, salaries and honorariums and other legitimate expenses — we create a support base for evangelism. Blindly putting money into the collection plate, however, is not good stewardship. We must be sure, without being too critical or analytical, that our shepherds spend the budget properly and that they do not compromise the vision of the church.

As a policy and practice, I have always supported the local church. Quite frankly, however, I have found that a lot of churches are not worthy of that kind of support and confidence. Many congregations have become so self-centered and introspective that they have little or no outward witness. They do not preach the gospel; they show little or no interest in the things that concern the heart of God. They place no emphasis on training in discipleship and evangelism. Having lost their first love, they are neither the "salt of the earth" nor the "light of the world."[7] Hundreds of thousands of our surveys reflect this spiritual impotence: 50 percent of the members are not sure of their salvation, 95 percent do not understand the ministry of the Holy Spirit, and 98 percent do not regularly share their faith in Christ.

Our Lord said, "When the Holy Spirit has come upon you, you will receive power to testify about me with great effect, to the people in Jerusalem, throughout Judea, in Samaria, and to the ends of the earth, about my death and resurrection."[8] The church that is not seeking to reach its Jerusalem and extending its outreach to the uttermost parts of the earth is disobedient to the Great Commission of our Lord. Life is far too short and dollars far too limited to try correcting a church or denomination that is unfaithful to our Lord's command to disciple and evangelize from our Jerusalem to the uttermost parts of the earth.

In assessing our giving to the local church, we must ask ourselves these questions: Is the holy, inspired Word of God being proclaimed from the pulpit and in the community without compromise? Does the church have a world vision and a fruitful witnessing outreach into its own community? Is the church training disciples to help fulfill the

Great Commission? If the local congregation is not walking in the power of the Holy Spirit, is not committed to its true biblical task, and is not willing to be influenced in this direction, it does not deserve our investment of time or money.

The church staff. The Word of God also gives us the responsibility to meet the needs of those who minister the gospel. "It is written in the Law of Moses," the apostle Paul records, "'You shall not muzzle the ox while he is threshing.' So also the Lord directed those who proclaim the gospel to get their living from the gospel."[9]

Meeting the needs of those who minister should be on a level "worthy of God."[10] Christian workers should be paid adequately to care for their needs. Forcing them to live in poverty or allowing them to enjoy the lap of luxury is not good stewardship. Providing for them in such a way that they have enough for their own needs and "plenty left over to give joyfully to others"[11] pleases God.

Caring for our Christian leaders may often extend beyond the term of their active service. A church in the midwest learned that a former pastor had terminal cancer and that he and his wife were living in a substandard apartment in another state. Both were elderly and could not work, yet they maintained a loving and godly attitude. Concern for this man stirred among the congregation as they remembered his faithful service to them many years before. When they learned of the couple's needs, they took a collection to help them financially. The congregation stayed in touch, providing for other needs and encouraging this couple through his sickness.

Later that year, the church celebrated its centennial. The minister and his wife attended a few of the festivities, even though he was too ill to preach. Joyfully, many of the members embraced them, grateful for their faithful service and dedicated leadership.

World missions. Giving to missions is a vital part of a steward's commitment as well. I believe that at least half of the church budget should be designated for missions. Dr. Frank Barker of Briarwood Presbyterian Church in Birmingham, Alabama, has for twenty-eight years led his congregation in dedicating 50 percent of their annual budget to missions. The late Dr. Oswald Smith, pastor of the famous People's Church in Toronto, Canada, said, "I would not pastor a church that would not give 50 percent of its budget to missions."

I would encourage every Christian to participate in the missions program of his church. However, a faithful steward should not channel his entire missions budget through the local body. The cause of Christ is much bigger than a single congregation's outreach. One should save a reasonable amount of whatever the Lord entrusts to him to help such groups as The Navigators, InterVarsity, Young Life, Youth for Christ, Child Evangelism, World Vision, Fellowship of Christian Athletes, Campus Crusade for Christ, various Bible societies, and others. An extension of the church, these ministries touch the lives of tens of millions around the world with the gospel of Christ.

When you give to missions, think of investing dollars where they will help introduce the largest number of people to Christ and build them in their faith so that they in turn will win and disciple others. Select groups worthy of trust, then give of your time, prayers and financial resources to help them fulfill the Great Commission.

Priority Four: Society

Putting God first in our finances involves yet another priority—helping nonbelievers see the life-changing power of Jesus Christ as a result of our involvement in society, and ministering to the physical needs of God's children.

Helping nonbelievers. As a faithful steward, one should be a constructive member of secular life. Caring for the poor, the orphans and the widows, participating in the local PTA, and giving of our time, talent and treasure to agencies concerned for the welfare of the community is a godly responsibility. It is possible for a Christian ministry to be so involved in its worldwide strategy that it neglects local opportunities for service.

I frequently remind our leadership, "We need to be active in different civic groups and community projects where we live because in so doing we show that we are good citizens, and we become 'salt' and 'light' for our Lord in these situations."

Although we should spend our primary funds on the direct evangelism of the world, we must not isolate ourselves from society in our evangelistic endeavors and thus become insensitive to its needs. Rather, as the apostle Paul admonishes, "While we have opportunity, let us do good to all men . . . "[12] thereby showing forth the love of Christ and opening the hearts of people to the gospel.

Ministering to God's children. Contributing to the physical needs of our brothers and sisters in Christ also brings glory to our Lord. Paul said, "Let us do good to all men, *especially to those who are of the household of faith.*" Christians all around us are hurting for compassionate help in times of distress.

A few years ago, Larry and Gail, a young rural couple, became Christians. Excited about serving the Lord, they grew rapidly in their spiritual walk, joyfully putting God first in every area of their lives. Soon, however, the couple faced a serious problem that challenged their faith.

Larry farmed with his father. As he shared Christ with him, his father angrily gave Larry an ultimatum to either renounce his faith or lose his share of the farm machinery in their partnership. Gently but firmly, Larry went on serving God despite his father's opposition.

With the high price of machinery and labor, Larry knew he could never afford all that he needed for the next spring's planting. He and Gail prayed about their situation and determined they would never go back on the commitment they had made to the Lord. Together, they informed Larry's father of their decision and then waited confidently to see what God would do.

The Christian farmers in the area united in prayer over Larry's situation. When they saw that he was without the means to put in his crop, they worked out a plan to help him. They loaned him equipment and bought diesel fuel, seed, and other necessary items. They gave freely of their time and labor to help Larry do his spring work in spite of their own long workdays.

Larry's potatoes and sugar beets were planted on time and the harvest that fall was good. For three years, he received help from these farmers until he no longer needed assistance.

As a result, the small community in which Larry lived was changed. People took note of the love and care that these Christian families had shown for each other. Many joined small group Bible studies and some eventually accepted God's love and forgiveness in their lives. The loving care of these neighboring farmers also inspired other Christians in the community, encouraging them in their faith.

The sacrificial giving of these farmers showed that God was first in their lives. As His steward, have you put Him first in your finances? Are you setting priorities to accomplish that goal?

Our Lord said, "Blessed is that servant whom his master will find so doing when he comes."[13] As we obey His command to faithful stewardship, we too will receive the

commendation of the Master. What a joyous reunion that
will be when He returns!

For Reflection, Discussion and Action

1. Prayerfully ask the Holy Spirit to help you set financial
priorities. Write them down and review them each time you
make out your bills or do your accounting.

2. Examine your giving to missions to see if it reflects the
priority you have set for it.

3. Set aside a personal fund solely for those in need. Ask
God to guide you in meeting their needs.

4. I wrote in this chapter: *An individual who neglects his
family's needs in order to give much to many organizations
and causes is a poor testimony to the love and care that our
heavenly Father has for His children.* How can you balance
this with the tendency to over-indulge loved ones? How can
you tell which way you lean?

9

Motives for Giving

When Jerrod felt the basketball hit his palms, he faked a drive to the middle, easily eluding the six-foot hulk guarding him. He drove down the baseline, his legs pumping under him like oiled pistons. Reaching under the basket, he flipped the ball with perfect spin. As it sailed up, right on target, he felt that familiar surge of pride roll through him.

Suddenly, he crashed into a defending player, his feeling of power vanishing as he lost his footing. He stumbled and sat flat on the floor, missing the sight of his ball as it hit the top of the square on the backboard and bounded through the hoop.

The referee's whistle, sharp and brittle, cut through the cheers of the crowd. Jerrod stood up, unhurt, as the buzzer signaled the end of the game for him. It was his fifth foul. Anger flashed inside him against the referee but he controlled himself and strode to the bench. His substitute dashed by, eager for his chance to play.

As Jerrod sat sullenly on the bench, the coach leaned over and spoke with a resigned tone, "You took it in your own hands again."

A Christian and the star of his team, Jerrod rested his head dejectedly in his hands and watched the play resume. Too many fouls! His hopes for receiving the "Mr. Basketball" award at the end of the tournament were fading. The game no longer seemed important to him. Instead, his mind focused on one thought — the award. Did he still have a chance to win?

Once ahead by twelve points, his team slowly lost ground to within two points of a tie. *Maybe the coach was right,* he mused. *Maybe I'm not a good team player. I guess I just want to become Mr. Basketball.* He glanced at each one of his team members on the court. None of them would win awards, yet they played with all their strength.

The teams flew down the court, and suddenly the game was tied with two minutes to play. The gym exploded with cheering on both sides. Resolving to put his selfish interests behind, Jerrod began to stamp his foot in time to the cheers.

"Get this one!" He clapped loudly as the player who substituted for him drove for a lay-up. When the ball went through the hoop, he stood and raised his fist in the air. "Way to go, Aaron!"

As his team pulled ahead, point by point, he yelled and cheered. "Keep it up! We've almost got it in the bag!"

When the final buzzer sounded, the team had won by ten points. Jerrod dashed out onto the court with the rest of the chanting fans to engulf the sweaty players. "We're number one! We're number one!" Setting aside his preoccupation with the trophy, his only thoughts were of the championship game tomorrow night and how the team would go on to play their best.

Jerrod is not unlike most of us. In all areas of our lives, we are often driven by motives that may not always be clear.

Good stewardship involves more than the mere knowledge and application of the principles and priorities of giving. Motives are essential parts of the picture as well. They determine our reasons for giving. Built upon the right attitudes, our motives will generate the kind of giving that pleases God and brings glory to His name.

By scrutinizing our reasons for giving, we may find both wrong and right motives.

Wrong Motives for Giving

Have you ever seen old boxcars standing idle, rusting on the railroad tracks? Once they were valuable components of the transportation system. When they were no longer needed, however, they were switched onto a sidetrack and abandoned to stand useless and empty.

Our giving can resemble those boxcars. Since our goal in stewardship is to put God first, we start with good intentions. We give faithfully. In addition to the local church budget, we contribute to missions and respond to the needs of the poor. Somewhere along the line, however, wrong motives cloud our vision. Losing sight of the purpose of our stewardship, we become ineffective, unfruitful and useless to our Lord.

In the Book of Acts, Luke relates the example of Ananias and Sapphira. Many had laid gifts at the apostles feet for the care of the needy. They brought the entire amounts from the sales of their lands and houses. Ananias and Sapphira also sold their property and handed their gift to the apostles. Wanting to look as generous as everyone else, yet keep a portion for themselves, they misrepresented their contribution as the full proceeds of the sale. "While it remained unsold, did it not remain your own? And after it was sold, was it not under your control?" Peter confronted. "Why is it that you have conceived this deed in your heart?

You have not lied to men, but to God."[1] Their deceit exposed, Ananias and Sapphira died at the apostle's feet.

Peter did not rebuke them for giving only a part of their profit, but for lying. Their untruthfulness and wrongful motives had made their gifts unacceptable to God.

We may masquerade our improper motives so skillfully that they take on the characteristics of sincerity, but we cannot hide these hollow and sinful purposes from the One who sees all.[2] As we examine our motives, let us be aware of the subtle ways in which we, too, can misrepresent our giving.

To Manipulate God

In recent years a distorted view of stewardship has emerged in Christian circles. If you give, the theory suggests, God *must* repay you up to a hundred times the original gift. The assumption is that, since God's law of sowing and reaping is predictable, one can manipulate it like a bank account. Lifting scriptures out of context to lend credibility to this concept, its proponents make it sound logical and convincing. However, this give-to-get hypothesis has disillusioned many Christians who have not experienced the abundance they expected.

Although God promises a return of up to a "hundred fold" to His faithful stewards, He cannot be bribed, manipulated or blackmailed into it. The apostle Paul asks, "Who could ever offer the Lord enough to induce him to act?"[3] In God's economy, getting is the *result,* not the goal, of our giving.

To Fulfill a Whim

Christians donate millions of dollars every year to organizations which appeal to their heart-strings through emotions or high-pressure Madison Avenue tactics. Many worthy ministries, meanwhile, lack sufficient funds to operate because their appeal is not popular enough. Giving that rides on such an emotional roller coaster achieves no objectives and sets up a dangerous hit-and-miss pattern that displeases God.

A purposeful steward does not give emotionally but considers the need prayerfully and carefully. He does not let a whim dictate his actions, but appropriates the wisdom and power of Almighty God to achieve much for the kingdom.

To Relieve Guilt

Guilt motivates people to do many things. Attempts to give their way into God's favor to hide their neglect of spiritual matters are common. But the dollar has buying power only in temporal matters. The currency of the kingdom is not cash but obedience. Giving out of guilt ultimately leads to feelings of frustration and failure because such stewardship does not please our heavenly Father. God is looking for stewards who, with a pure heart, apply His Word to their daily lives.

To Increase Self-Worth

One of the misfortunes in the body of Christ today is the preoccupation with self. Volumes of books have been written and many sermons have been preached on the need for personal fulfillment and a better self-image.

A healthy self-concept is, of course, vital to one's fruitfulness as a witness for Christ. The knowledge that God views us as holy and righteous and totally forgiven, that we are free from condemnation because of what Christ has done for us, should inspire us out of gratitude and as an act of obedience to share His love and forgiveness with everyone who will listen. The emphasis on self-glorification, however, has resulted in spiritual feebleness, leaving much of the body of Christ introspective and unfruitful.

The desire for a sense of self-worth motivates the stewardship of many Christians, who believe their generosity makes them look good in God's sight and in the eyes of the church. However, because the focus of such giving is on themselves, they live empty and fruitless lives.

Like sowing poor seed in unfertile soil, giving for the sake of feeling good about ourselves can never be productive.

To Achieve Recognition

Another wrong motive for giving is recognition. Ananias and Sapphira tried to impress others with their liberality. They thought they could buy a reputation for being generous. The consequences of their deception, however, were severe. Not only did they lose their lives, but the Scriptures also record their infamy for all to see, generation after generation.

Recognition in itself is not wrong. I often acknowledge and express my gratitude to people for their giving—not to exalt them, but to encourage them to share their testimony with others. Giving for the sake of recognition, however, leaves a pathetic legacy. Charles Kingsley wrote, "If you wish to be miserable, you must think about yourself, about what you want, what you like, and what respect people ought to pay you. Then to you nothing will be pure. You will spoil everything you touch; you will make sin and misery out of everything God sends you."

To Gain Power

The lust for power drives some to give. Often churches and other Christian ministries face the problem of a donor trying to control them with a sizeable gift. A member of a church, for example, may give his pastor a new car or the down payment on a luxurious new home. The member may use his gift to gain a position of influence over the pastor and favored status in the church.

Some donors try to buy their way into leadership. Acts 8:17-24 records how Simon offered money for spiritual power. As a sorcerer he had enjoyed great influence and prestige because of the things he could do. Simon gave up his sorcery to follow Christ, but he still had a thirst for power.

As Peter and John laid hands on the people to receive the Holy Spirit, Simon was envious.

"Let me have this power, too," he pleaded, "so that when I lay my hands on people, they will receive the Holy Spirit."

The apostle Peter's response to such motivation applies equally today. "Your money perish with you for thinking God's gift can be bought!" he exclaimed. "You can have no part in this, for your heart is not right before God."

In verse 23, the Amplified Version calls Simon's motive "the gall of bitterness and a bond forged by iniquity to fetter souls."

To Gain Tax Advantages

The temptation of Christians in the higher income brackets is to regulate their giving for maximum tax advantage. Indeed, good stewardship requires that they avail themselves of every legal tax exemption available. Giving additional sums to the work of the Lord before the end of the year is sound financial planning. A true test of their motives and faithfulness in stewardship, however, is whether they would continue to give if the government were to drop deductions for religious and charitable giving.

The goal of giving, we have seen, is to put God first in our lives. If we give merely for the tax deduction, our motive is wrong. By focusing on our own gain, we rob God of His glory and our giving is unfruitful.

Are your reasons for giving pleasing to the Lord Jesus? I encourage you to examine your motives. Ask the Holy Spirit to reveal any wrongful attitudes. Then confess them and ask Him to empower you to give with a pure heart.

Right Motives for Giving

Godly motives for giving stem from a cheerful, loving heart committed to a heavenly view of gain. The apostle Paul wrote:

> Godliness is a means of great gain, when accompanied by contentment. For we have brought nothing into the world so we cannot take anything out of it either.[4]

In this passage Paul emphasizes timeless values. Godly motives produce eternal fruit. How we handle our money actively indicates our purpose—whether heavenly or earthly in giving.

To Express Love for God

We cannot find a more pure motive for giving than to express our love for God.

The apostle John writes, "We know love by this, that He laid down His life for us; and we ought to lay down our lives for the brethren. But whoever has the world's goods, and beholds his brother in need and closes his heart against him, how does the love of God abide in him?"[5] If we truly love the Lord Jesus, we will be sensitive to those who are close to His heart—the poor, the orphans and the widows, and those who have not yet accepted the gift of God's Son.

A few years ago, Vonette and I decided that at Christmas time we would give to someone who had a real need instead of buying gifts for each other. During the recent holidays, just before Christmas, we called several people who work in an inner city ministry here in San Bernardino to ask if they knew of anyone who needed help. We learned about a woman whose husband had just left her with four children. A couple days later, we heard that the son of a former staff member had been killed in an accident, leaving his wife and children. Helping these precious people was far more meaningful to us than placing presents for each other under our Christmas tree. We didn't give because we wanted spiritual "Brownie points," nor were our hearts set on a heavenly reward. We gave because the love of God shed abroad in our hearts constrained us to reach out in compassion to them.

To Please God

A second reason for giving is to please God. The apostle Paul exhorts, "Our aim is to please him always in everything we do..."[6]

One Sunday morning an excited little girl gave her pastor $4.32 for missions. "How did you get so much money?" he asked, surprised.

"I earned it by collecting rainwater and selling it to the washerwomen who live on the edge of our town," she smiled proudly. "They paid me two cents a bucket! Now I want to send a missionary to tell boys and girls about Jesus."

The amazed pastor took the money and asked, "Shall I say, 'A gift from Mary'?"

"Oh, no!" Mary shook her head firmly. "I don't want *anyone* to know but Jesus. Put it down as rain from heaven."

When our motives in giving are pure, as little Mary's were, they focus all the attention on the Lord Jesus. Nothing motivates me more in life than pleasing my heavenly Father who is holy, sovereign and omnipotent, and who loves me so much. As I consider the sacrifice that He gave through His Son, Jesus Christ, my heart overflows with gratitude. I would rather come into the presence of my Lord at the end of this earthly journey and hear Him say, "Well done, good and faithful servant,"[7] than to be the richest man in the world. More lasting than the highest recognition and praise of men would be my Lord's commendation, "Bill, I am really pleased with you. You were obedient. You honored Me. You brought glory to My name." Those words would remain for eternity. What else can compare to that?

To Lay Up Treasures in Heaven

Many Christians miss the special blessing of God because they do not obey our Lord's command recorded in the Gospel of Matthew:

> Don't store up treasure here on earth where they can erode away or may be stolen. Store them in heaven where they will never lose their value, and are safe from thieves. If your profits are in heaven your heart will be there too.[8]

Motivation is a key factor in accumulating heavenly wealth. Jesus knew that by storing up treasures on earth, we would soon take on the appearance of the world. Through selfish desires, we would cease to reflect the character of God and seek our own glory. By laying up treasures in Heaven, on the other hand, we would declare the glory of His kingdom.

Everything we do to bring men and women into the kingdom of God, every act of kindness, every expression of love, is laying up treasure in God's storehouse. We must give out of love for God and our gratitude for His love and sacrifice through our Savior Jesus Christ. Having given with such love, what a joyous privilege it will be one day to lay our treasures before the feet of our wonderful Lord.

To Be a Channel of Blessing

God has given us the awesome privilege of channeling His abundant resources to a desperately needy world. As instruments to accomplish His will, we will never lack anything for the task. Dr. H. C. Morrison, a famous Holiness Methodist preacher, was walking along a busy street one day when he received a five-dollar bill from a stranger. "Thank you, friend," Dr. Morrison smiled as he resumed his walk. Soon he met a poor widow. Knowing her need, he gave her the five-dollar bill that the man had just given to him.

A few minutes later as the preacher continued his walk, another stranger pressed a five-dollar bill into his hand. Dr. Morrison soon met another needy person and felt strongly impressed to give the second five-dollar bill to him. This time, however, he decided to keep the money for himself.

"Strange to say, that was the last gift of five dollars I received that day," Dr. Morrison said. "I believe God would have continued the chain of money coming to me as I walked along if I had passed it on."

The chorus of a beloved old hymn goes like this:

> Make me a blessing, make me a blessing
> Out of my life, may Jesus shine.
> Make me a blessing, O Savior, I pray.
> Make me a blessing to someone today.

Do these words express the desire of your heart? Is your purpose in giving to "be a blessing to someone today"? How exciting to be able to sing this song with fullness of heart for the glory of God! How thrilling to be a channel of God's resources for furthering His kingdom here on earth!

To Help Reach the World for Christ

God considers "an immortal soul beyond all price.

There is no trouble too great, no humiliation too deep, no suffering too severe, no love too strong, no labor too hard, no expense too large, but that it is worth it, if it is spent in the effort to win a soul."[9]

A leader of a large international ministry once said, "We have the master plan to reach the entire world for Jesus Christ . . . all we need is the money!" Accomplishing this task is a huge undertaking. Billions of dollars are needed. I know of scores of missions that say they could reach the world with the gospel if they had enough financial support. As faithful stewards, our primary financial responsibility is to help worthy ministries reach the largest number of people for Christ possible.

Our Lord's last command before He ascended into Heaven was, "Go and make disciples of all the nations..."[10] How important are His final words to us as stewards? We can answer this question only by examining our hearts — and our checkbooks — to see if our stewardship truly furthers His kingdom. Maintaining right motives through the power of the Holy Spirit is an urgent task if we are to accomplish this objective to the glory of God.

In the preceding pages we have been preparing for our adventure in giving. We have considered the qualifications, attitudes and responsibilities of a steward. We have surveyed the biblical principles that form the basis and define the goals of stewardship. We also have examined our motives in giving. Next, let us look at an often controversial approach to giving which has been the cornerstone of Christian stewardship for centuries — tithing.

For Reflection, Discussion and Action

1. List the wrongful motives for giving. Using Psalm 139:23,

24, examine your heart to see if any of these motives typify your giving. Then list the right motives and ask the Holy Spirit to help you exemplify each of these in your life.

2. Explain why it is important to have right motives in giving.

3. Share a recent incident of giving in your life. What was your motive?

4. If you had witnessed the death of Ananias and Sapphira, how would you have felt? What does this story say to you personally about the importance God places on motives?

5. How does handling money show a giver's purpose? Think of an example that illustrates this principle.

Part 3

God's Plan for Supernatural Giving

10

Tithing: Addressing the Controversy

One afternoon, Grandpa Clark strode into his house, pockets bulging with treats for his grandchildren. As he settled into his creaking rocker, the children clamored around him with expectant faces, each pushing and shoving so he could be first to see what Grandpa had brought them.

The gray-haired man dug deep into his pockets and pulled out a fistful of candy, handing each child his favorite kind of treat. When he finished, he leaned back in his rocker with a smile of contentment to watch them tear at the wrappings.

On his left, two jealous brothers argued over whose flavor of lifesavers tasted better. Another child sat at his feet munching a candy bar. Suddenly, a tiny red-haired sweetheart patted her grandpa on the arm. Concern furrowed her brow.

"Would you like some of my M&M's, Grandpa?" she asked with sad, shy eyes. "You don't have anything."

Grandpa Clark peered down at his only granddaughter and grinned. Gently, he gathered her dainty form into his lap. "Why, you haven't even opened your candy," he observed.

She stared into his eyes with a frank expression. "'Cause I want you to have the first one."

"Why, thank you, I think I will," he smiled, carefully tearing open her little package. With relish, he removed a couple of colored candies and popped them into his mouth. Then he wrapped his arms tightly around her, engulfing her happy face.

This story brightly illustrates tithing—giving back to God the first part of what He has given to us.

When did tithing begin? For what purposes was it established? Has it accomplished these objectives for God's glory? Some Christian leaders argue that tithing is an Old Testament custom that inevitably leads to unscriptural giving in a modern world. Is tithing for today? Or has the church resorted to an outmoded tradition to finance its endeavors?

In the coming pages you will learn the biblical answers and discover the deep significance of tithing in stewardship. But first, let us examine the controversy surrounding the practice.

Arguments Against Tithing

The word *tithe* itself comes from an Old English term simply meaning *a tenth*. However, Christian leaders use *tithe* in two different senses. To some, *tithe* means the general giving of a tenth of one's income or resources to God. To others, *tithe* refers to the specific manner of funding God's work mandated by Mosaic Law. I use *tithe* in the first sense.

Opponents of the practice offer several reasons for their resistance, some of whom merely argue against the

Mosaic tithe, not tithing in general:

1. Tithing is based on law, not grace
2. Tithing depends on the Levitical priesthood for application
3. Christ did not tithe, so neither should His followers
4. Tithing serves materialism
5. Tithing promotes non-participation
6. Tithing is a device to raise money

Let's examine each argument for a moment.

Tithing is based on law, not grace. The Mosaic Law required the Israelites to give three tithes, each for a different purpose:

1. *The Levitical tithe* — to support the clergy and the needs of God's work
2. *The festival tithe* — to demonstrate God's priority in their lives
3. *The poor tithe* — to care for the poor and needy

Since tithing funded the Jewish theocracy, tithing was equivalent to our modern-day tax structure and financed government salaries, funded social and religious systems and provided a welfare system. Tithes were compulsory, not voluntary.

The usefulness of tithing depended on the national life of Israel. When the Mosaic system of government ended with the destruction of the temple and the final dispersion of the Jews, so did the tithe.

Under the New Testament, grace replaced the Law. The early Christians struggled with this issue. Jewish believers tried to bind Gentile Christians to the old system, but the apostle Paul taught that the Law did not have dominion over the church. "If you are led by the Spirit," he asserted, "you are not under the Law."[1]

If God did not command Christians to keep the Law, He did not compel them to tithe either. Christ fulfilled the Law with His death on the cross, nullifying its tyranny and replacing it with the freedom of grace. To require tithing would remove the precious liberty we have in Christ.

Tithing depends on the Levitical priesthood for application. During the Mosaic period, the Levites received the tithe and distributed it among the children of Israel. Without their specific offices, the tithe cannot be valid.

God established the tithe to ensure the Levites an inheritance and to pay them for their services.[2]

Christ, on the other hand, provided a far better priesthood. The apostle Paul elaborates:

> For the Law appoints men as high priests who are weak, but the word of the oath, which came after the Law, appoints a Son, made perfect forever.[3]

Since Christ's priesthood replaced that of the Levites, it also nullified the support system for this old order, part of which was the tithe.

The manner of tithing mandated by Mosaic Law depended entirely upon the existence of the Levitical priesthood. If the priesthood were to end, as it did when Jesus Christ became our eternal High Priest, the tithe would also end.

We must conclude, therefore, with the sealing of the New Covenant at Christ's death, the tithe passed with the system of which it was a part.

Christ did not tithe, so neither should His followers. During His ministry on earth, Christ exhorted His disciples to follow His example.[4] When we walk in His footsteps, we desire to make His priorities ours.

The New Testament does not say that Jesus tithed. Although He discussed the subject twice, He did not command His followers to tithe nor give any precedent by doing so Himself.

One can assume, therefore, that the absence of tithing from Jesus' specific teachings gives mute testimony that its validity ceased with the end of the Old Testament.

Tithing serves materialism. Hiley Ward argues this point:

> If the American people are as materially minded as sales figures of recent years indicate, then a minimum standard in giving is certainly welcomed. It is perhaps harsh to say that tithing is the fruit of a materialistic suburbanism, but tithing, with a minimum in giving, is clearly compatible with the mid-century "suburban emphasis," or the rapid spending of one's income on material things.[5]

When one seeks to obtain the most materially, tithing fits smoothly into his system of budgeting. Proportionate giving relieves the donor of any pressure to give more, thus freeing the greater part for himself. With his gift paid out, he can sit back, relax, and not feel guilty about how he spends the other 90 percent.

Tithing promotes non-participation. Tithing resembles a professional baseball game. The stands fill with spectators who sit back to watch eighteen players bat a ball. The fans never participate in the sport, but pay to watch their heroes win for them.

Similarly, tithing turns a steward into a spectator of church life. After giving a proportionate amount to finance the "action," the giver sits back to watch the results. He does not get personally involved and prefers to remain anonymous in the stands.

This non-participation may come slowly. At first, the

tither envisions the feats that his contribution will accomplish. As time goes on, however, his vision blurs. When the collection plate passes, he drops in his money with little thought about how it will further the cause of Christ. Soon, he worries more about padded seats and new carpets than about outreach programs.

Tithing is a device to raise money. Some religious organizations develop the logic: If tithing works, let's use it to get our share of the donation pie. If we have insufficient funds to finance our programs, let's push tithing and our contributions will increase dramatically.

Instead of teaching the practice because it helps direct godly stewardship, many churches and organizations wield proportionate giving as a device to make their stewardship departments more effective. Using guilt to motivate constituents, they raise massive funds for their causes. Their misuse of tithing makes this method of funding one to avoid.

Arguments for Tithing

Denominational councils and parachurch organizations variously state their views on the subject. Among them, advocates of tithing substantiate their case with weighty premises.

1. Tithing is a practical guideline for systematic giving

2. Tithing provides spiritual release

3. Tithing acknowledges God as the source and owner of all that we possess

4. Tithing is a voluntary act of worship

5. Tithing teaches us to put God first

Let us now examine the first two arguments.

Tithing is a practical guideline for systematic giving. The apostle Paul emphasized this when he exhorted believers: "On the first day of every week let each one of you put aside and save, as he may prosper . . . "[6] In 2 Corinthians, he again implores:

> Let each one do just as he has *purposed in his heart;* not grudgingly or under compulsion; for God loves a cheerful giver.[7]

Paul realized that systematic, purposeful giving ensures consistent stewardship. Without a functional plan, we fall prey to our whims. One day, we feel excited about giving, the next we may forget. Even worse, we may not feel like giving at all. A practical plan for giving, however, enables us to circumvent the emotions and circumstances that would hinder us from being faithful stewards.

What could better achieve this goal than the tithe? Originated by God, it has helped to build up His kingdom and further the cause of Christ for centuries.

Tithing provides spiritual release. Spiritual blessings are incomparably superior to material ones. When a steward gives the first portion of his income to God, he receives an abundance of joy and peace. R.T. Kendall writes:

> Tithing is one way to find great spiritual release. Sooner or later we come face to face with this matter and the failure to walk in the light results in a greater bondage than ever. But when one enters upon the life of faithful tithing there is a sweet release to be experienced that cannot be fully explained to another person. This release by itself is enough to convince one fully how serious God is about this matter of tithing. The peace and joy are so wonderful that a frequent reaction is a kind of sorrow that one had not been doing it sooner.[8]

When we hang on to our possessions, they own us.

Tithing releases us from the tyranny of materialism and clears the channel for God's abundant blessings.

As the debate over the legitimacy of tithing fills religious magazines and books on stewardship, one wonders, *How do we address this controversy in the light of God's holy, inspired Word?* To answer the critics and consider the remaining arguments of proponents, we must search the past.

For Reflection, Discussion and Action

1. What is your understanding about tithing? Describe your view in a short paragraph.

2. Do you agree or disagree with the arguments against tithing? With the arguments for tithing? Why?

3. What do you think would happen to a tither who is not totally committed to God? Why?

4. Discuss how cheerful giving can be done systematically.

5. Do you think it is important to give God the first part? Why?

11

Tithing:
The Historical
Foundation

From ancient times man has recognized his duty to offer a portion of his substance to God. Even pagan religions practiced this custom.

Records dating from as far back as 3000 B.C. show that the Egyptians tithed the spoils of war to their gods.[1] The Pharaohs and many of their people annually gave the first fruits of their crops to the temple. On festival days, they gave offerings of precious gems, fruit, vegetables, game, salt, honey, even beer and wine. The proportions may have been as much as a sixth but not less than a tenth of their increase.[2]

Other early civilizations — the Babylonians, Phoenicians, Arabians and Chinese — also gave a percentage of their income to pagan gods. Representing the whole profit they received, the number ten had a mystical significance for them.[3]

The ancient Greeks and Romans, too, left historical

records of tithing. Their mythology and documents transcribed from the oldest writers and lawgivers provide examples of the practice. Considering it a duty toward their gods, the Greeks and Romans regarded as sacrilege any withholding of the tenth. Many other ancient societies also practiced tithing throughout Europe, Africa and Western Asia.

What is the significance of its prevalence in early civilization? Henry Lansdell explains a possible reason for this phenomenon:

> When grammarians and philologists observe that many words of a class . . . linger in use among peoples widely separated, and having no visible connection with one another, these students of comparative tongues infer, that at some time in the remote past, the ancestors of such peoples must have lived together, and spoken such words in a common language.[4]

A Common Root

Since tithing is traceable among various cultures throughout ancient history, it must have had a common root. Let's examine its beginnings briefly.

No doubt the concept of tithing existed in the mind of God even before the creation of man, for "all things have been created through Him and for Him . . . and apart from Him nothing came into being that has come into being."[5]

From the start, God embedded a vital principle in giving which remains basic to tithing today: *attitude*. The sacrifices of Cain and Abel exemplify this.

We assume by the reference to their sacrifices that God had ordained them following the fall of Adam. Matthew Henry comments:

> We may conclude that God commanded Adam, after the fall, to shed the blood of innocent animals, and after

their death to consume part or the whole of their bodies by fire. He thus referred to that punishment which sinners merit, even the death of the body, and the wrath of God, of which fire is a well-known emblem, and also prefigured the suffering of Christ.[6]

Having attached such vital importance to these sacrifices, God could not take lightly their offerings. Cain, who tilled the land, placed the fruit of the ground on his altar. His brother, Abel, who raised sheep, sacrificed the firstlings of his flock. God spurned Cain's gift but accepted Abel's. Here again, Matthew Henry offers insight:

> The offerings of Cain and Abel were different. Cain appears to have approached God in a way of his own devising, and despising that which God had appointed. He came in his own name, without the acknowledgment of his sinfulness . . . and not to supplicate mercy, but only to thank God for the blessings of his providence. In so doing he manifested a proud, impenitent, unbelieving heart. Therefore, he and his offering were rejected.
>
> Abel brought a sacrifice of atonement . . . He came as a sinner, according to God's appointment; by his sacrifice expressing humility, sincerity, and believing obedience. Thus seeking the benefit of the new covenant of mercy, through the promised Seed, he was accepted according to that covenant.[7]

The contrast in this story illustrates how God regards attitude. The example of Cain shows the futility of trying to change inward sin with self-willed pious action. The beauty of a heart overflowing with thankful obedience, however, shines like a jewel through Abel's life. Throughout history, this principle plays a foundational role in the practice of tithing.

Examining the Old Testament Record

With this background, let us now consider the remaining arguments for tithing and how these principles counter the views of those who oppose tithing.

Tithing acknowledges God as the Source and Owner of all that we possess. Early biblical records date the origin of the tithe to Abraham. He gave a tenth of his spoils of war to Melchizedek, the King of Salem and the priest of the Most High God.[8]

Returning victoriously from a battle, Abraham joined Melchizedek in giving God the glory. Melchizedek brought out wine and bread and blessed Abraham. In response, Abraham gave the priest the first portion of his spoils in public testimony of God's ownership over his possessions.

As the spiritual father of every Christian believer,[9] Abraham set an example for us to follow.

Tithing performs a role opposite that of mere giving, which suggests that we own all that we possess. Through tithing we acknowledge that God created our increase. As stewards of what God entrusted to us, we set aside a proportion to use for the cause of Christ. We never consider any part of the amount to be our sole property but prayerfully tithe on the entire amount.

When we give out of our own generosity, on the other hand, we take the credit for ourselves. We imply that the responsibility for the gift lies with our own efforts. We donate a little here — to this person or that one, contribute a little there — to this cause or that. A selfish spirit infects our giving, and we impress others that we are the masters of our faith and of our possessions. Only those who tithe in the biblical way truly glorify God with their gifts.

Tithing is a voluntary act of worship. At Bethel Jacob affirmed his commitment to God by pledging his tithe.

> "If God will help and protect me on this journey and give me food and clothes, and will bring me back safely to my father, then I will choose Jehovah as my God! And

this memorial pillar shall become a place for worship; and I will give you back a tenth of everything you give me!"[10]

We, too, should tithe as an act of worship to the One Who blesses us. Through this act, we keep our focus on the heavenly Father and testify to His kindness and generosity toward us.

Jacob's family grew into a mighty nation and needed divine statutes to govern its new home in the Promised Land. What the children of Israel had given voluntarily, God now required to fund the new theocracy. Whenever Israel gave from a heart of gratitude and worship for God's provision, tithing brought blessing and prosperity.

Tithing teaches us to put God first. Moses said, "The purpose of tithing is to teach you always to put God first in your lives."[11]

As Israel established itself in the Promised Land, the people prospered. God blessed their obedience and subdued the godless tribes living in the land. Soon, however, the children of Israel lost their first love for the God of their fathers. They began worshipping the idols of the pagans they defeated.

Their material prosperity or impoverishment directly reflected their spiritual attitudes. Whenever they put God and His commandments first, the children of Israel enjoyed peace and abundance. When their hearts turned away from Him, God chastised them.[12] Israel followed this pattern throughout its history.

We can learn from this lesson. How often have we conceived grand strategies for giving, only to find that the money we intended to give vanished in day-to-day spending? Covetousness, greed, and frivolous buying all tempt even the most dedicated Christian. When budgets stretch unmanageably or a crisis depletes the paycheck, many Christians skimp on their tithe to cover a personal deficit.

God does not honor a gift that comes from the leftovers. As we have seen earlier, He requires the first and the best of our increase.[13] Tithing ensures this.

The children of Israel not only scorned God's laws but neglected their tithes. Malachi warned them of the disastrous consequences of their disobedience,[14] but they had lost the spirit of giving that springs from a heart overflowing with love toward God. Tithing, when practiced, had fallen into legalism and eventually ceased, only to be revived and forsaken again — thus creating cycles of tithing that have reached from biblical to modern times.

In light of the biblical record, let us now look at three of the six questions raised by those who oppose tithing. Although not specifically addressed here, their remaining arguments are considered conceptually throughout the book.

Is the practice based on law and therefore not binding under grace? Does the tithe have validity apart from the office of the Levitical priesthood? Did Christ tithe, and if not should we follow the custom today?

Tithing in the New Testament

By Jesus day, four hundred years after the close of the Old Testament, tithing had become merely a religious duty that served as a vehicle for self-commendation. The Old Testament age had marked the beginning and the end of the first of three major cycles in tithing, each starting with the introduction of the practice and ending with its decline into legalism. The times of Jesus and the New Testament church would witness the genesis of the second cycle.

Our Lord mentioned the tithe twice during His ministry. In the first reference, He denounced the scribes and Pharisees for tithing meticulously without showing justice, mercy, and faithfulness to those around them.[15]

In the second mention,[16] Jesus related a parable of two

men, one who tithed pompously for self-glorification, and another who humbled himself when he realized his sinfulness. Our Lord condemned the Pharisee for his pride and commended the sinner for his humility.

Although our Lord did not command His followers to tithe in these passages, He did not disapprove of the practice either. For our Lord, the issue of giving did not center on the method. Realizing that the religious leaders had distorted tithing into a tyrannical set of rules, He turned the issue from how much a disciple should give to his attitude toward giving. His challenge went beyond written ordinances to loving "the Lord your God with all your heart, and with all your soul, and with all your mind, and with all your strength."[17] Love, gratitude and humility, not law, should motivate our giving. In this teaching we see the rebirth of the principles upon which the tithe rests.

Tithing, we have seen, did not originate with the Mosaic Law. The patriarchs tithed long before Israel became a nation. Since the principle precedes the Law, the fact that God compelled Israel to support the Levitical priesthood and fund the theocracy with their tithes has little bearing on the continued validity of the practice.

Even under Mosaic Law, the legal requirement to tithe did not excuse the giver from a godly attitude in stewardship. Solomon counseled, *"Honor* the Lord with your possessions, and with the firstfruits of all your increase."[18] To him the issue was not the Law. Tithing transcended the Law to the lofty heights of wisdom, respect, esteem and reverence. In his view tithing was an act of homage to the Most High.

Under grace, everything we have is a gift of God. All we have belongs to Him. We tithe, therefore, not as a requirement of the Law, but as an act of loving obedience and worship. By applying the wisdom of Solomon to our giving, we testify to our dedication to godly stewardship.

Giving 10 percent to the work of the Lord is a realistic starting point for a steward who wants to honor and glorify God with all his resources. As Dr. J. B. Gabrell declared, "It is unthinkable from the standpoint of the cross that anyone would give less under grace than the Jews gave under law."

The theory that our Lord did not tithe also is insupportable. Although the Scriptures do not *state* that He tithed, we cannot argue such a conclusion from silence. John, the beloved disciple of Jesus, wrote:

> There are also many other things that Jesus did, which if they were written one by one, I suppose that even the world itself could not contain the books that would be written.[19]

By using the argument of silence, we could also contend that our Lord *did* tithe, and that since the practice was so obvious, the writers of the New Testament saw no need to record the fact.

Let us remember that God ordained the practice. Christ saw no need to re-establish what He had never revoked. Furthermore, let us remember what Jesus told the Pharisees: "Render to Caesar the things that are Caesar's, and *to God the things that are God's.*"[20] Here our Lord reaffirmed their responsibility to pay taxes *and* give tithes.

Before our Lord ascended into Heaven, He gave His followers the Great Commission to spread the gospel throughout the world and make disciples of all nations. How would the early church founded by the apostles finance such a far-reaching task? Could the tithe be a means for accomplishing this mission?

What did the early Christians believe about tithing? From the Book of Acts through Revelation, little is mentioned about the subject. Most of the leaders in the New

Testament church came from Jewish backgrounds and probably tithed before their conversions. Whether they continued the practice we do not know. We assume they did from Christ's affirmation of the custom, and because they enthusiastically fulfilled the purposes of the tithe. They:

1. Provided for the needs of God's work

2. Declared God's pre-eminence in their lives

3. Cared for the needy within their own congregations and sent financial relief for believers in other cities[21]

We do know this: Measuring their giving by the grace of the cross and not by the legalism of the Law, the early Christians did not limit themselves to the tithe. They gave much more. Acknowledging God's ownership of all their possessions, they gave with an abandonment produced by love. In so doing, whose example did they follow?

The apostle Paul admonished the believers in Corinth to give "On the first day of every week . . . as he may prosper."[22] Although not specifically calling it the tithe, he instructed them to give regularly and proportionally according to their incomes — measures basic to the principle and practice of tithing.

We can be certain that if New Testament Christians tithed, they did so in the Spirit of Christ to help fulfill the Great Commission and not from a sense of obligation. What they put aside each week for the furtherance of the gospel signaled their return to the principles of giving which God established in the tithe: a humble attitude, an acknowledgement of God as the source and owner of all their possessions, a focus on worship, and a demonstration of His pre-eminence in their lives.

Early Christian Era

As the fledgling church grew explosively, church fathers struggled over its financial needs. How would they teach the steadily growing number of new believers to put God first in their giving? As poor city dwellers, many of the converts needed help from their Christian brothers. Furthermore, the number of clergy mushroomed. Their support required an organized method for collecting and distributing funds.

By the third century, the Old Testament practice of tithing seemed a proper solution to these problems, so the church fathers encouraged the tradition. Cyprian, Ambrose, Augustine, Jerome and Chrysostom publicly approved the system.[23] Tithing gained official status when the first Christian emperor, Constantine, endorsed it with an edict in the year A.D. 322.

The Christian world gladly embraced tithing in their enthusiasm for giving. Using it as a practical standard for stewardship, the masses voluntarily gave to the cause of Christ.

Pre-Medieval and Medieval Tithing

By the fifth century, however, abuses had crept into the system as the spiritual emphasis shifted from grace to law. Churchgoers no longer gave joyfully out of a sense of love and worship, but to achieve merit through works.

What had begun as a means of furthering God's work, and thus to help fulfill the Great Commission, slowly degenerated into a religious obligation. Again, the practice of tithing was pressing toward the end of another cycle. Several developments combined over the next few centuries to deepen this legalism. In 567 the Synod of Tours recommended that Christians donate 10 percent of their property to the church. In 585 the Second Council of Macon converted their recommendation into a church tax, citing excommunication as the punishment for non-payment. Although these assemblies represented only a portion of the church, they accurately depicted its course.

Two popes, Leo the Great and Gregory the Great, also helped spread legalistic tithing. Making it compulsory, Leo set aside special days during the year for the people to bring their offerings. During his pontificate, Gregory declared these collections a mandatory church tax.

Meanwhile, the call to tithe came from the remote corners of the church in Europe. Recognized legally in England as early as 786, the practice prevailed during the reigns of Alfred, Edgar, and Canute. Converted Lombards copied the custom from their northern neighbors. As they conquered parts of Italy, they brought back to Italy their practice of bestowing special merit on those who tithed. This heightened an already enthusiastic fervor over tithing among the Roman clergy.

All that lacked in this pre-medieval society to make tithing compulsory throughout Europe was a strong secular leadership. The Carolingian kings, culminating in the reign of Charlemagne when he conquered Italy, accomplished this feat.

By placing collections in the hands of the clergy, Charlemagne created power struggles between the ruling kings and the church.

In time secular power became subservient to the church. The papacy strengthened its hold over the state with forged documents claiming that early Christians paid tithes to the apostles and thereby to the popes, who traced their line back to Peter.

Many perversions of the tithe arose, including the vending of indulgences (to escape punishment for sins) and the buying and selling of church offices. As the clergy enriched themselves with these and other abuses, they lost sight of the purposes for which they had revived the tithe. No longer did collections further God's work, care for the needs of the clergy or provide for the poor. Instead, contributions amassed huge riches for the church. As a result, the laity begrudged paying their tithes.

Seedbed of the Reformation

The Reformation of the 16th century sprang from the seedbed of lay dissatisfaction and the many religious abuses of the church. Quakers, Separatists and Anabaptists resisted paying tithes, insisting that giving should be voluntary.

Even in the New World, church leaders had enacted compulsory giving into law. As opposition to abuses produced by involuntary tithing deepened within the church in Europe and America, tithing was either abandoned or changed in its form. Intellectual and political climates changed worldwide, permitting secular control in countries formerly dominated by religious rule. State churches turned their tax control over to governments. Anticlerical revolutions against the Roman Catholic Church forced it to seek other avenues for revenue.

By the 18th century, ecclesiastical authorities in the New World rescinded involuntary church tax laws and replaced them with new strategies for fundraising. The new system included the rental of pews, lotteries, subscription lists, church-farm ownership and the sale of goods within the church.

Joyful Worship to Binding Legalism

For nearly 1,500 years, tithing had dominated church funding. At first it served the body of Christ well to help bring the Good News to the world. As centuries passed, however, the practice degenerated to an unrecognizable state tax. Tithing no longer resembled the Mosaic pattern, nor did it maintain the spontaneous, joyful custom of the early Christians from which it had grown. Failing to glorify God, the practice began to fade until it virtually disappeared. Ironically, tithing had made the second complete cycle from joyful worship to binding legalism, which had characterized the Jewish system through the Old and New Testament periods.

Once again, the tithe no longer fulfilled the purposes for which God designed it. The clergy collected funds far beyond their needs, manipulating the tithe to amass wealth. The tither lost sight of the pre-eminence of God while giving to man-made monuments. The poor and needy found themselves impoverished even more under its tyranny.

Rejected by the body of Christ, tithing seemed doomed to a hapless future. Was it unworkable as a means for helping to fulfill the Great Commission? Was it a useless and misshapen practice that could never glorify God? Was it so prone to abuse that it could never accomplish the purposes which God intended?

As a spiritual awakening swept Europe and America in the late 18th and early 19th centuries, tithing would again be debated throughout the evangelical world.

For Reflection, Discussion and Action

1. Discuss the difference between "giving" and "tithing." Which one describes your practice and why?

2. List the three purposes for the tithe. In what ways could your giving help achieve these purposes? Be specific.

3. Even though the individual Israelite was commanded by law to tithe, did this relieve him from having the right attitude in giving? Why?

4. Discuss why giving must be done:

    a. With a humble attitude

    b. To acknowledge God as source and owner of all possessions

    c. With a focus on worship

    d. As a demonstration of God's pre-eminence in our lives

5. Check your attitudes in giving. Do you give freely or under compulsion? At what times or which places does your giving most resemble godly stewardship? Least? How can you make your attitude glorify God in your weak areas?

12

Tithing in a Modern World

Like a lantern whose oil supply runs dangerously low, the spiritual flame of the 17th century church flickered and dimmed. Chilling waves of stiff orthodoxy and cold dogmatism solidified and cooled the volcanic fervor unleashed by the Reformation.

Emphasizing right thinking and human reason, church leaders gave little attention to salvation and Christian experience. Tithing also had ceased to be a vibrant part of Christianity.

Society reflected the hollowness within the institutional churches. Protestants and Catholics vied among themselves for political power while secularized professionals replaced the clergy as policy makers within many governments. Pulling people away from the church, materialism and nationalism reached into all levels of society.

As the church entered the 18th century, her flame burned even lower. New threats to her life came from all sides. Rationalism with its emphasis on knowledge, deism and its foundation of human reasoning, social philosophies hostile to supernatural experiences, unscriptural theories derived from scientific developments—all robbed the vitality from many denominations. Religious wars between nations and dissention among religious groups dampened enthusiasm for the cause of Christ. All these pressures caused church memberships to dwindle and fostered serious doctrinal errors within established denominations.

Western civilization paused on a spiritual threshold. Swirling secular and anti-religious forces, building up steam against the church, weakened her witness for Christ. Her message sounded hollow and impotent. The practice of tithing languished deep in the valley of legalism, enriching the coffers of cold institutions. The future of the church looked bleak.

Could the Holy Spirit turn the tide of spiritual coldness and again raise up a force of godly soldiers committed to fulfilling the Great Commission? How would He equip His army with the needed finances for the task?

Great Movements of the Holy Spirit

Even while the church slipped further into tepid religiosity, God was rebuilding His army. A tiny movement of Pietists sprang up among Lutherans in Germany. Its founders, Philip Spener and August Francke, rejected the prevailing attitude that the Christian life consisted solely of memorizing catechisms, attending services, and partaking of the sacraments. Emphasizing the new birth and a deep devotion and active service to our Lord, these Pietists formed a center of spiritual renewal at the University at Halle. There they gathered a group of converted students to train them for the ministry.

Deeply committed to the power of prayer, Francke trusted God to provide enough funds to support the outreaches he started. With little money of his own, he opened an orphanage and sent missionaries to India, to America and to the Jews. God honored his faith, and donations poured in from all over Germany.

In their missionary zeal, the Pietists did not rely on church taxes to finance their endeavors. Rather, they committed themselves to depend wholly on the Lord. A renewed attitude of love for God and devotion to evangelism spawned godly perspectives in giving. Within this small fellowship of Pietists, the Holy Spirit began to raise a company of believers who would humbly dedicate their resources for the service of their Savior. Their selfless attitudes started the first rumblings of a mighty work of God, which eventually bore fruit in great worldwide efforts to reach the lost for Christ.

Before dying out in the first half of the 18th century, Pietism passed on its fervor for evangelism to the Moravian church. The Moravians expanded Pietism's passion for the lost and distinguished themselves as the first Protestants to seriously undertake the Great Commission.[1]

As missionaries, they supported themselves and endured many hardships to bring the gospel to lands far beyond their little settlement in Germany. Through prayer and selfless giving, they exemplified the godly principles of stewardship modeled by the Pietists.

They gave all of their possessions in the service of the Lord Jesus Christ. Motivated solely by His sacrificial love, they acknowledged God as the source and owner of everything they had. They made giving an act of worship and through their commitment to the Great Commission showed His pre-eminence in their lives.

Moravian missionaries planted the seed of the gospel in John and Charles Wesley during a voyage to America to become missionaries to the natives. Their example and message inspired both John and Charles Wesley to experience a personal salvation through faith in Christ. For John this occurred at Aldersgate when he read Martin Luther's treatise on faith in the introduction to Luther's commentary on the book of Romans. Immediately after his conversion, John Wesley visited the founder of the Moravians, Count von Zinzendorf, to learn more about their spiritual fervor. Although he did not accept everything the Moravians believed, John eagerly embraced their love for Christ and the selfless giving that his mentors so ably manifested in their lives.

He returned to England with a new vision to evangelize the lost. Teaming up with George Whitefield, the Wesley brothers preached to the masses. They used open air evangelism anywhere they could find an audience to preach the gospel and denounce the gross sins of coarseness, brutality, immorality and drunkenness that were rampant in the society.

Through their efforts, the rumblings of spiritual renewal erupted into sweeping movements of the Holy Spirit. In the Great Awakening of the last half of the 18th century, George Whitefield conducted seven preaching tours across the Thirteen Colonies in the New World. His spiritual influence touched the hearts of our founding fathers and led to the convictions which insisted on freedom from England, resulted in the Revolutionary War, and gave birth to the Declaration of Independence and the Constitution of the United States.

In England this revival kindled a similar movement through the preaching of John Wesley called the Evangelical Awakening. This surge of spiritual growth among lower and middle classes eventually led to the formation of the Methodist Church.

A practical man as well as a spiritual leader, John Wesley taught his converts that yielding all one's possessions to God is basic to biblical stewardship. In his sermon, *The*

Use of Money, he urged:

> Gain all you can. Save all you can. Give all you can.
> You are a steward; therefore provide modestly for your
> own wants, and give the surplus. Do not stint yourself to
> this or that proportion. Render unto God, not a tenth,
> not a third, not a half; but all that is God's, so that you
> may give a good account of your stewardship.[2]

John modeled this principle by his own life. He lived
on a modest income and gave away the rest, leaving nothing behind at his death except his clothes, his books and his
carriage.

Student movements for evangelism, Bible and mission
societies, new denominations, and Christian organizations
rose up in the 19th century from the fertile soil of these
revivals.

Tithing Revived in the 19th Century

By the 19th century, the Holy Spirit had laid a firm
groundwork upon which to build the advancing church.
Even though the intensity of the earlier awakenings had
diminished, they had established a legacy of revivalism.

In the early 1800s, a Second Evangelical Awakening
spread throughout America, Britain, the European Con-
tinent and elsewhere among the Baptists, Methodists and
Presbyterians. Tens of thousands of new converts joined
their ranks. The renewal sparked the founding of seminaries and colleges, added midweek prayer meetings and
Sunday schools to churches everywhere, and created a fervor for missions.

As this revival lost some of its momentum, Charles
Finney began conducting meetings in New York State. His
greatest fruit came in the fall and winter of 1830-1831 when
one thousand people received Christ through his preaching. By today's comparisons, that number would represent

tens of thousands.

D.L. Moody carried the revival spirit into the last quarter of the century, beginning his ministry in the army camps during the Civil War. Emphasizing the love of God and calling for repentance, he eventually preached to millions of people during evangelism campaigns in the United States and England.

The 19th century revivals added hundreds of thousands of new converts to the churches. This growing army of new believers in Europe and America began to voice urgent concern for the social and political ills created by the democratic and industrial revolutions. As a result, Christian agencies opened medical dispensaries, built orphanages, and provided relief for the poor. They demanded prison reform, women's suffrage, and the abolition of slavery. They also influenced the regulation of industry and the organization of labor unions.

The fresh zeal and vitality from this spiritual fervor sparked the formation of many mission and Bible societies, including the American Bible Society, the American Tract Society, and the American Sunday School Union. The founders of these groups had a single vision — furthering the kingdom of God. Bible societies provided materials to educate believers and to evangelize non-Christians. New Bible colleges and seminaries trained workers to help fulfill the Great Commission. Mission organizations in Europe and America sent hundreds of workers into foreign fields to preach the gospel.

As in the past, the burgeoning church sought direction in managing the new financial challenges before her. Although contributions flooded into the church to help finance the evangelization and discipling of the lost, she urgently needed a systematic pattern of giving to meet the pressing demands of the expanding body of Christ. Tithing once again surfaced as the answer.

Thomas Kane, an enthusiastic supporter of the tithe, led the way in 1880 by mailing pamphlets to evangelical leaders across the United States. He encouraged them to re-establish the tithe among their constituents.

In 1896 he joined The Tenth Legion, an organization formed to encourage tithing. Helping to revitalize the league, he saw it grow from 5,000 to 18,500 members by 1902.[3] In 1904, he helped organize another group called The Twentieth Century Tithers' Association of America.

Tithing Spreads in the 20th Century

Rising from the ranks of the laity, the practice of tithing has grown rapidly in the 20th century. As a result, many denominations and Christian groups have formed stewardship departments to encourage systematic giving. The Student Volunteer Movement, instrumental in challenging many young men to accept the call to the foreign mission field, produced a missionary statesman, John R. Mott, who strongly promoted tithing. He once said that if Americans would put their tithes on the altar of Christ, the gospel could be preached to every person on the earth.[4]

The practice of tithing has spread around the world since Thomas Kane first promoted it. Alliances, confederations, councils and other coalitions among churches and religious groups have exchanged ideas for stewardship which include tithing.[5] As mission societies have seen the need to encourage systematic giving in new churches, they have recommended tithing. Churches even outside of the western world that did not have a legacy of tithing have adopted the method after assessing its strengths.

Thus we have seen the beginning and rise of the third cycle of tithing.

Is tithing for today? I believe it is. Contributions to religious organizations in the Unites States alone approximate $40 billion a year.[6] With the responsibility that huge sums of money brings, the body of Christ urgently needs the direction that tithing gives to stewardship.

By following the biblical principles underlying the tithe, we will be faithful stewards of the resources God entrusts to us. Let us not allow the debate over tithing to rob us of the joyous adventure of giving systematically to further the cause of Christ, and thus help accelerate the fulfillment of His Great Commission.

For Reflection, Discussion and Action

1. Discuss how your understanding of tithing has changed since reading the history of tithing.

2. In your opinion, why did tithing rise from the laity rather than the clergy?

3. Describe how tithing has been used and misused throughout history.

4. Imagine that a new Christian has asked your opinion about tithing. How would you answer him?

13

Tithing Your Time and Talents

Does the principle of tithing apply equally to our time and talents as it does to money?

How much of our time should we set aside for the work of the Lord?

How are you using the time God has given you? Are you investing your abilities and skills for His glory?

Time is the heritage of every person. Whether a king or street sweeper, an astronomer or truck driver, a business tycoon or a grocery clerk, each of us has the same number of hours.

Many necessities and opportunities demand much of our day. Our work takes a large slice of life. Being a good husband or wife, father or mother, requires time. Our bodies and minds need good nutrition, exercise, recreation and leisure. We must get the proper amount of sleep.

As Christians, we have spiritual priorities as well. How many hours or days in a month should we set aside for evangelism and discipleship and the ministries of our church? What about caring for the poor, the orphans and widows as our Lord commanded?[1]

With all these tasks competing for time, how can we balance our responsibilities to fulfill our temporal and spiritual duties?

Setting priorities and managing time are not new concepts. Many management experts have written or talked on the subject. As we discussed in a previous chapter, good stewards must manage their time wisely.

Let me suggest a way to accomplish this task that Christians seldom consider today—tithing your time and talents.

Tithing Your Time and Talents

We have already examined several basic principles behind the tithe. Let us review four of them briefly.

1. Tithing reflects a thankful, obedient attitude
2. Tithing acknowledges God as the source and owner of all that we possess
3. Tithing is a voluntary act of worship
4. Tithing teaches us to put God first

How do these precepts apply to tithing our time and talents?

A godly attitude is foundational to all stewardship. As with money, God prizes those who give of their time and talents cheerfully. Our Lord receives no glory when we minister begrudgingly or merely out of duty. A faithful steward serves because he has a heart for God. He labors lovingly, gratefully and obediently.

As we have seen, stewardship involves more than our material resources. Everything we have is a gift from God. Every second of every minute, every minute of every hour, twenty-four hours a day, belong to Him. He gives us our abilities and the strength and wisdom to use them, and He holds us accountable for the way we manage these precious gifts.

The stewardship of our time and talents must not stop with the mere doing. Whether teaching a Sunday school class or taking a meal to an elderly shut-in, all we do must flow from a heart filled with praise and worship. Dedicating ourselves to the work of the Lord in this manner pleases Him and opens the channels of His blessing in our lives.

Although God's Word does not specifically require us to tithe our time and talents, our Lord did command us to put Him first in all things. "Don't worry at all about having enough food and clothing," He said. "Your heavenly Father already knows perfectly well that you need them, and he will give them to you if you give him first place in your life and live as he wants you to."[2] Tithing our time enables us to give God priority and assures that we will fulfill our service to Him.

How to Tithe Your Time and Talents

Giving ten percent of our time to the work of the Lord is not a burdensome task. Many of God's dedicated children give far more. Let me share several steps you can take to begin the process.

First, *evaluate everything you do.* You may be surprised at how much time you already give. Take out a large sheet of paper and list all your activities. Let me suggest a few possibilities:

- Studying God's Word daily
- Spending time in private and group prayers
- Teaching or attending a Sunday school class
- Attending worship services
- Leading a home Bible study

- Sharing God's love and forgiveness with a neighbor, friend or stranger
- Discipling someone to share his faith in Christ
- Preparing a meal for a shut-in
- Comforting someone who has just lost a loved one
- Singing in the church choir
- Visiting a sick person in the hospital
- Reading your child a Bible story
- Caring for the spiritual needs of your family
- Showing hospitality to new neighbors
- Tuning up a single mother's car
- Taking a fellow worker to lunch as a witness

The list is endless. I'm sure you can add many more. Now estimate the time you spend per day, week or month on each project.

Next, examine the rest of your calendar. How much time do you waste on selfish pursuits? Do you squander many hours watching television programs or reading books that have no edifying merit or spiritual benefit? Are you using your time and talents in selfish leisure or personal pleasure beyond your reasonable needs? How much of this time can you dedicate to the work of the Lord?

Second, *arrange your priorities*. Group your schedule into blocks of time: daily, weekly and monthly. Take advantage of the less busy moments to increase the time you devote to God's work. Weave ministry into your daily, weekly or monthly routines. Be flexible. Set realistic goals. With love and gratitude to our Lord, strive to give at least ten percent of your time to His work.

Third, *identify your talents*. Do you sing? Play a musical instrument? Bake? Perhaps you are a carpenter, landscaper, engineer, mechanic or bookkeeper. You may have a talent for sewing, organizing a group meeting, teaching or writing. Your skill may be typing, photography or painting. Ask God to show you how to use your talents for His glory.

Finally, *find creative ways to use your abilities*. List the ways in which you can serve. Opportunities to devote your time and talents are limitless. Your ministry may be one of helps. Perhaps you could spend an hour or two a week vacuuming, washing dishes, dusting and making beds for an elderly couple who cannot care for their own home. Maybe you could babysit the pastor's children while he and his wife call on members of the church. Or you could take a handicapped friend or neighbor to the supermarket. What a testimony to the love of God your efforts would bring!

My brother Forrest is a building contractor and retired Air Force Colonel. His wife Betty is an artist and has painted scores of beautiful oils. Both constantly seek to help others as a ministry to the Lord. For example, as a labor of love they donated several hundred hours remodeling my office and the board room at the international headquarters of Campus Crusade. They give generously of their time to help many staff members remodel their homes.

Let me ask you two vital questions: What is the greatest thing that ever happened to you in your entire life? What is the most important thing you can do to help another? Wherever I have asked these questions, the answers are always the same. "Knowing Christ is the greatest thing that ever happened to me, and sharing Christ with others is the most important thing we can do for them."

If this is true, we must prioritize our time to introduce as many people to Christ as possible and help them grow in their faith. You will be amazed at the number of openings you will find to give your testimony, to lead a Bible study, to hold an evangelistic dessert in your home, or to share Christ with a fellow employee during lunch. All you need to do is ask God to help you plan strategically to reach your loved ones and neighbors for Christ.

Art De Moss, one of the busiest executives I have ever known, invested much of his life in the kingdom of God. Art didn't waste time. Often, as we talked together, he would busy himself with important business documents needing his attention. Although he had a heavy schedule, he spent many hours telling others about the Lord and discipling those he led to Christ. He wrote them letters, sent literature and talked to them on the telephone. In the latter years of his life, he probably spent more time on evangelism and discipleship than he did in his business.

Clarence Brenneman is a successful businessman in Oregon. Many years ago, he and his wife attended a Lay Institute for Evangelism at Arrowhead Springs. Through this training, Clarence learned how to witness and led his first person to Christ. As this joyful couple began to lead many others to the Lord, they came back for more training. Eventually, they joined the associate staff of Campus Crusade to hold Lay Institutes for Evangelism themselves.

I'm sure this godly couple gives more than 50 percent of their time to the cause of Christ. They have trained tens of thousands of laymen to witness for our Lord. A pastor called me one day to testify, "There are 1,200 of us taking a week of training under the leadership of Clarence and Vida Brenneman. We want you to know that our church and the city will never be the same because of the way God is using them to help all of us understand how to become more effective witnesses for our Lord."

The Blessings of Tithing Your Time and Talents

Opportunities to invest ourselves in the lives of others will come our way as we make ourselves available. Along with these opportunities comes abundant joy.

A dear friend, Ben Jennings, flew to Hong Kong recently. As morning dawned on the Pacific, he noticed his young Chinese seatmate reading a book that looked like a Bible. Ben struck up a conversation with him, hoping to share his faith. "Do you speak English?" he asked, smiling.

"A little," the man nodded.

"Are you a Christian?"

"Not yet."

"You're reading a Bible," Ben observed.

"It belongs to my mother." He pointed to a little woman sitting on the other side of him. "She wants me to read it."

Handing him a Chinese translation of the Four Spiritual Laws, Ben invited him to read the booklet. When he finished, Ben asked, "Does it make sense to you?"

The young man nodded. "Yes. It does."

Since Ben doesn't speak or read Chinese, he guessed where the prayer to receive Christ was located in the booklet: a page past the diagram containing the two life-identifying circles. He pointed out the paragraph to him. "Would you like to pray that prayer right now?"

"Yes."

"Pray it out loud," Ben instructed. "Make it your own prayer to God as you read it."

The young man repeated the prayer softly. Then Ben followed with a prayer of thanksgiving for the wonder of the moment.

Ben wanted to make sure the young man had understood his decision. "Where is Jesus now in relation to you?" he asked.

"In here." He pointed to his heart.

"Would you like to thank the Lord now for coming in? He would love to hear you."

"Can I pray in Chinese?" the young man wondered.

"Yes, you can."

Although Ben could not understand his words, the man's sincerity was clear and beautiful. When he finished, Ben looked at him. "Could you tell your mother what you have just done?"

With a smile, the son turned to her. The only part of their long conversation that Ben could understand was the mother's gasp of joyful surprise.

The Chinese woman spoke no English. From there on into Hong Kong, however, she used clear international body language. Each time she caught Ben's eye, she clasped her hands, grinned from ear to ear, and bowed repeatedly.

"I experienced two joys that morning," Ben says. "The excitement of introducing that young man to Christ and seeing the gratitude of his praying Christian mother will live long in my memory!"

Abundant joy is only one of the blessings of tithing our time and talents. In the law of sowing and reaping, we discovered that planting a seed produces a bountiful harvest. Like begets like. If we plant corn, we reap corn. If we sow wheat, we harvest wheat. This principle, we saw, applies to giving. Whatever we give by faith, we reap. And we always reap more than we sow.

How does this relate to time and talents?

I challenge you to give a tithe of your day, week or month to the Lord. You will be amazed at how much more you will accomplish in the remaining nine-tenths. Results will show in various ways. God may help you increase your efficiency. Others may offer to help you with a time-consuming project. The demands on your time may lessen.

I encourage you to tithe your time and talents for six months to see how God will multiply and expand the hours He has given you. As you faithfully do so, you will discover that your natural and spiritual gifts will increase in fruitfulness. You will strengthen your talents or even discover new ones.

My good friend Arlis Priest discovered this secret many years ago. I received a letter from him recently. In it he shared how God had abundantly blessed him for devoting 50 percent of his time to the work of our Lord.

In 1962 he had joined twenty other businessmen who met with me about the decision to buy the Arrowhead Springs property, now the international headquarters of Campus Crusade for Christ. "I was so impressed with your vision," he wrote, "that I decided to donate a year of my time to help refurbish the property so you could continue in the spiritual ministry with your staff."

It took us several months to purchase the property. When the time came for Arlis to fulfill his commitment, he had spent all the money that he had in reserve for that year. Nevertheless, he decided by faith to keep his promise.

Arlis and his lovely wife Nadine sold their home in Phoenix and moved to Arrowhead Springs. As manager of the property, he worked eighteen to twenty hours a day for the next year.

"An amazing thing took place after we returned to Phoenix," he wrote. "Within thirty days, I sold a large apartment project and made almost as much money as I would have had I worked the full year.

"I was so moved by God's financial blessing that I decided to donate the first 50 percent of my time to God, then trust Him for the last 50 percent to make a living. Believe it or not, I made as much during the half month as I did before while working the full month. That went on for the next twenty years."

God is generous to every servant who sincerely places Him first. He will give back to us many times over everything we offer to Him out of gratitude and love.

Let us dedicate our time and talents, as well as our treasure, to help fulfill the Great Commission and uplift the Body of Christ until our Lord returns.

For Reflection, Discussion and Action

1. List ways to tithe your time and talent that can be worked into your present schedule.

2. Determine what blocks of your time are wasteful. How could you use them to serve the Lord?

3. List your talents and estimate how much time per week you spend using them for the work of the Lord.

4. In which areas can your church use your talents?

5. Prayerfully look for new opportunities to share your faith with others.

Part 4

Steps to Financial Freedom

14

God Wants You to Be Financially Free

"You can have complete financial independence . . . today!"

Have you ever responded to one of those enticing newspaper advertisements? What a wonderful prospect!

In July of 1903, a young man moved to Chicago intent on making his fortune. With only a few years of experience working with dairy products, he determined to set his theories about cheesemaking into operation.

Starting his enterprise with only sixty-five dollars in his pocket, a cart, and a rented horse named Paddy, he worked hard selling cheese direct to Chicago retail merchants. By the end of the first year, he was $3,000 in debt. Soon he could get no credit to purchase more cheese and had to run his business day-by-day as he could pay cash.

He worked harder. Still, success eluded him. Finally, one day he loaded his wagon determined to sell more than $100 worth of cheese. When he counted the money from his sales at the end of the day, however, he had taken in only $12.65. He turned Paddy toward home, dazed and beaten.

"Paddy, what's the matter with us anyhow?" he asked the horse dejectedly.

Paddy's ears laid back, and out of the air the young man seemed to hear the answer, "You are working without God!" He stopped the horse and looked around, but could see no one. As he sat wondering, he realized that he had left God out of his business. Right there, he determined to make Him a partner.

The man who made this momentous decision was J.L. Kraft, founder of the Kraft cheese company. The Lord blessed his commitment and within a few years the company owned more than fifty subsidiaries with operations in Canada, Australia, England and Germany. Today, Kraft is a household word in dairy products.

I met Mr. Kraft, a humble, godly man, in Hollywood in the 1940s at a meeting for businessmen. His example of stewardship is a model for us all. He began tithing when he earned barely twenty dollars a week and continued investing in God's work throughout his life. Sometimes he donated more than one-third of his income to the cause of Christ.

Mr. Kraft achieved financial freedom through wise business practices and by applying biblical principles of stewardship. He not only supported his church, but helped further religious education. He also gave liberally to home and foreign missions. Although God has blessed many of His children with wealth, most of us can only dream about financial independence. Financial freedom, however, is for every Christian steward who faithfully follows God's plan for giving, saving and spending.

Financial freedom means having enough to provide adequately for our households and to give generously and joyfully to God's work. From the beginning, this has been God's plan. He has prospered those who have demonstrated good stewardship, showing themselves worthy of trust in spiritual as well as material things.[1] As men and women have proven faithful, He has made them channels of love and blessing.

God wants us to be financially free so we can put Him first in our life and give liberally to the advancement of His kingdom. He wants us to be sensitive to His voice, ready to follow Him whenever — and wherever — He leads. A difficult task when one is under constant financial pressure!

Whether or not we are willing to admit it, money worries drain us emotionally and spiritually. They rob us of creative energy. They steal our peace of mind and keep us from being fruitful disciples for our Lord. The average Christian, weighted down with payments and expenses, cannot give with joy and thanksgiving as God desires. Deaf to the voice of God, he does not hear when our Lord calls and does not see where He leads in his finances. Countless millions of dollars have been lost to the cause of Christ and His kingdom in this manner because unfaithful stewards have diverted funds for selfish fulfillment.

Why Christians Suffer Financially

If this is not God's plan, why do many Christians live in financial bondage? The reasons are basic. Not understanding or obeying scriptural principles of stewardship, they succumb to the world's philosophy of money. They shackle themselves with materialism and make little or no commitment to God's work.

Malcolm Muggeridge, one of England's leading intellectuals, came to our Christian Embassy headquarters in Washington, D.C., for lunch one day. Together we talked about the things of God. On that day, he offered little hope for the future of the Western world.

The love of money and the love of things is slowly

destroying the average person in America and in Western Europe, he explained. People are greedy, grasping for more than they have. Our appetites know no bounds; we have become insatiable.

As a result, he said, there is more vital Christianity in Eastern Germany than in Western Germany, in Poland than in Italy, in the Soviet Union than in England. The Christians who willingly pay the price of persecution in these countries have learned to seek first the kingdom of God and His righteousness and to be satisfied with what they have. With humility of heart, they join the apostle Paul in saying, "I have learned, in whatsoever state I am, therewith to be content."[2]

It is in the faithful stewardship of that which God entrusts to us, not materialism, that we find fulfillment and true meaning to life.

First and foundational, since Christ's church is like a body, every member must surrender to the head. Christ must be Lord of all areas of our being. The effective members in the body of Christ have made total, irrevocable commitments of their lives—including their finances—to the Lord Jesus. The ineffective members live as slaves to their greeds, wrongful attitudes, and improper priorities. Lacking commitment to God's work, they fail to give consistently, if at all.

To escape from the bondage of materialism they must deal with the sin of selfishness.

As faithful stewards, we will become world Christians. Nothing pleases the heart of God more than seeing His children involved in helping to fulfill the Great Commission by faithfully giving of their finances, prayers and yes, even their lives.

Myths About Money

A wrong concept about money also contributes to financial bondage. Some find virtue in poverty. Others measure success by capital assets and net worth. Whether poor or rich, they are slaves to mammon.

Three myths feed the poverty syndrome:

"Money is the root of all evil."

"To have money is sin."

"One must be poor to be spiritual."

Let's examine each of these for a moment.

Money is the root of all evil. Money itself is *not* the root of evil. "The *love* of money," the apostle Paul declared, "is a root of all kinds of evil, for which some have strayed from the faith in their greediness, and pierced themselves through with many sorrows."[3] Money is simply a medium of exchange. From God's perspective, only one's devotion to riches causes him grief.

To have money is sin. I do not believe that, as Christians, we should concern ourselves with how large our bank account is, or how big our home should be, or how prestigious our cars can look. Instead, our focus must be on how we manage the resources God has given us to invest for the cause of Christ. There is nothing wrong, however, with bank accounts, beautiful homes or nice cars. If every Christian lived in poverty, nonbelievers would not listen to what we have to say.

Many men of the Bible were wealthy. Abraham, Job and Solomon, for example. The Scripture teaches that "In the house of the righteous there is much treasure . . . "[4] and "As for every man to whom God has given riches and wealth, and given him power to eat of it, to receive his heritage and rejoice in his labor—this is the gift of God."[5]

Today God has blessed multitudes of committed Christians with wealth, which they use to help organizations like Campus Crusade for Christ win and disciple millions around the world for His kingdom.

The Holy Spirit used people of means to draw me to Jesus Christ. As a materialistic young nonbeliever, a happy pagan, I depended upon my own abilities. I had never met a Christian businessman whom I admired. When I moved to Hollywood, however, I suddenly found myself face to face with some of the most prominent Christian business and professional leaders in Los Angeles. One of them developed a good part of the famous Bel-Air, a prestigious residential community in Los Angeles. I discovered that they had nice homes—some of them elaborate—and that they lived a good lifestyle.

Although some of my newly found friends were wealthy, they did not attribute happiness to their lovely cars and beautiful estates. They lived for Jesus Christ only, and that gave me a whole new perspective on Christianity. I became receptive to the gospel because I met Christians who were successful. They taught me that one does not have to live in a dump or drive a jalopy to be a Christian. He can live well.

Whether wealthy or of humble means, we need the right perspective. Since everything belongs to God, what we have is not important; only what possesses us counts. True prosperity means having enough resources to accomplish what God calls us to do.

One must be poor to be spiritual. One's financial status does not necessarily reflect his spirituality. The apostle Paul is an example. He said, "I know how to be abased, and I know how to abound . . . "[6] In Paul's lifetime, he experienced both poverty and riches. He knew what it meant to go hungry and to suffer need. He also enjoyed the blessings of abundance. Through it all, the apostle wrote, "I have learned the secret of contentment in every situation."[7] This is the key to spirituality.

Some of the most godly people I know are among the most wealthy. Although worth millions, they are filled with the Holy Spirit and walk in the joy and wonder of our Lord's resurrection.

A poor person not committed to the Lord Jesus can be as guilty of wrongful motives and unbiblical attitudes as a wealthy one. Virtue is not inherent in poverty or riches. Our life does not consist in the abundance — or lack — of the things we possess.[8] God desires that we have enough resources to meet our needs and to carry out His will. Balance is the key. "Give me neither poverty nor riches," God's Word says. "Feed me with the food You prescribe for me; lest I be full and deny You, and say, 'Who is the Lord?' Or lest I be poor and steal, and profane the name of my God."[9]

These misconceptions have led many sincere Christians to suffer needless want, making it virtually impossible for them to help further the cause of Christ.

Equally binding are the myths which feed the success and wealth syndrome:

"Money provides security."
"Money brings happiness."

Money provides security. Everyone wants to be secure. From the time of our birth, we have an instinctive desire to feel safe. We love to be cuddled firmly in our mother's arms. We enjoy snuggling before a crackling fire on a cold winter's night. We hope for financial comfort in our sunset years. Throughout our lives, we strive for strength, pursue protection and concentrate on certainty. The lure of money tempts these innate desires.

Money is deceptive, temporary and corruptive. Verse

after verse in the Scripture bears this out. In His parable of the Sower, our Lord explained that the "deceitfulness of riches" chokes the Word and makes it unfruitful in our hearts.[10] Solomon observed, "When goods increase, they increase who eat them; so what profit have the owners except to see them with their eyes? The sleep of a laboring man is sweet, whether he eats little or much; but the abundance of the rich will not permit him to sleep."[11] "Riches are not forever,"[12] the writer of Proverbs records. Our Lord warned, "Do not lay up for yourselves treasures on earth, where moth and rust destroy and where thieves break in and steal."[13] The apostle Paul cautioned Timothy, "People who long to be rich soon begin to do things that hurt them and make them evil-minded and finally send them to hell itself."[14]

Money brings happiness. If this were true, some in the world would have cause for jubilation. Much of today's wealth is in the hands of the "platinum caste" — the world's estimated 129 billionaires. So fabulously rich, they can afford anything from gold-trimmed Rolls-Royces and titanic yachts to baronial homes and palatial castles.

Were the wealth of the world's ultra-elite moguls reduced to dollar bills, the resulting stacks of money would be mind-boggling.

The resources of Europe's biggest landowner, German billionaire "Prince TNT" von Thurn und Taxis, for example, would literally extend out of this world. Stretching 183 miles into the sky, his colossal fortune would tower a mere mile short of the spaceshuttle Discovery's orbit in September of 1988 — a height equivalent to thirty-three Mount Everests stacked one on top of the other.

The riches of Queen Elizabeth II of England easily eclipse those of Prince TNT, however. She holds $8.7 billion in the castle accounts, plus a jewelry cache considered one of the world's most splendid private collections. Her castle of cash would stretch 590 miles, virtually from the northern coast of Scotland to the southern tip of England.

The sultan of Brunei tops the list. The richest man in the world, his worth approximates a minimum of $25 billion. Almost everything in his Delaware-sized nation on the island of Borneo belongs to him. Valued at $300 million, his 1,788-room palace is crowned by two 22-carat gold-plated domes. According to professional wealth-watchers, the sultan could settle his country's debts, invest a billion a year, and splurge $100 million per year on himself without blinking an eye. His resources would form about 248 stacks of one-dollar bills reaching from the floor of the Mariana Trench (the deepest point of the Pacific Ocean, southwest of Guam) to the surface of the sea. Quite a sizeable sinking fund!

As outrageous as these fortunes seem, such wealth cannot guarantee happiness. Earthly riches never fully satisfy the heart. Rather, happiness stems from a vital relationship with God. I have discovered that individuals of modest means who love God generally experience the most contentment.

True wealth boasts in the knowledge of Christ and of His wonderful salvation, and in our dependence upon Him for the abiding riches that He bestows on all who believe and trust in Him.

A wealthy friend who lived near the Mexican border in the United States shared this heartwarming story. Once a week he would travel to Mexico to work with the poor. There he worked with a woman who was one of the most radiant, godly persons he had ever met. She lived in a small lean-to with a dirt floor. Her possessions were little more than a kettle, a knife, fork and spoon, and one change of clothes. She never had any food one day in advance of her need. Like the children of Israel in the wilderness, she received her "manna" each day. Yet she was always rejoicing and praising God for His goodness to her.

"I was a successful business man, with considerable wealth living in an expensive and beautiful home," my friend observed. "But she was obviously happier than I because she had to depend upon the Lord for everything."

Satan's Scheme

Throughout the ages Satan has schemed to distort, to enslave and to destroy. When God said, "Love," Satan said, "Hate." When our Lord said, "Have faith," the devil said, "Seeing is believing." When Jesus said, "Give," Satan said, "Get." In describing Himself as the Good Shepherd, the Lord Jesus addressed this conflict clearly.

> The thief does not come except to steal, and to kill, and to destroy. I have come that they may have life, and that they may have it more abundantly.[15]

The devil's tactics for leading Christians into financial bondage are varied and treacherous. Appealing to our senses, he emphasizes getting instead of giving, fosters covetousness over contentment, capitalizes on greed rather than need, and substitutes fear in place of faith.

God intended for material blessings to enable us to serve Him more freely and more fully. Satan knows the key to these blessings is giving. He aims to keep us from it, and thereby make us ineffective in our service to God.

I encourage you to obey God's Word, proving yourself a good steward worthy of His trust. Be sensitive to His voice, and be ready to follow Him wherever He leads. Enjoy the adventurous life of faith — a "faith that will not shrink, though pressed by every foe, a faith that shines more bright and clear when tempests rage without; that when in danger knows no fear, and in darkness feels no doubt."[16]

For Reflection, Discussion and Action

1. Discuss the difference between financial independence and financial freedom. Which can be most used by God? Why?

2. In which areas of your life do you feel greedy or materialistic? How have these feelings affected your spiritual well-being?

3. How can being a "world Christian" help you overcome selfishness? What steps could you take to make yourself more aware of needs around the world?

4. After re-examining the five myths about money, determine which one you are most susceptible to believing. Determine why it affects you.

5. Share one way in which Satan tempts you to give less. Be specific. How can you overcome this temptation in the future?

15

How to Be Financially Free

Karen stared at the divorce papers in her hands. Her life with Jim was over. Turning her head away from the stark black words on the white paper, she scanned the living room of her small apartment. Toys lay scattered everywhere. *Just like my life,* she thought. *Everything is in disorder.*

She and Jim had married almost ten years ago. At the time, they had high hopes for themselves. With a financial counselor, they had built a plan to make themselves financially secure. Jim had a good position with a stable company and kept moving up with a promotion every other year. She ran a profitable day-care business in the basement of their home, only taking time off to have their three children.

Over the years, they had built three new homes. Doing much of the construction as possible themselves, they would sell each as they completed it and use the profit to build a bigger one.

Two years ago, Jim's company transferred him to a managership several states away from their hometown.

The advancement meant an increase in salary and prestige for him. They sold their house, packed up their three children and moved. With part of their savings and the profit from the sale, they purchased a large home in an elite part of town.

Karen decorated, bought new furniture, and landscaped their new place. Then she settled in to enjoy the fruits of their hard work.

That's when she noticed how much she and Jim had grown apart. He never came home for supper anymore, gave minimal attention to their children, and spent lavishly to maintain his image at the office.

Then, one dark day, he announced his intentions to divorce her. Stunned, she pleaded with him and dragged him to counseling sessions with their pastor — all with no success. Finally, Jim packed some of his personal belongings and left.

Jim's extravagant spending habits and the expense of the divorce gradually depleted all they had gained over the past ten years. She watched as their grand financial plans crumbled into dust and sifted away. Selling the house and most of their lovely furniture to pay their debts, she rented a small apartment and found a job.

Now, with final divorce papers in hand, Karen surveyed her past. She and Jim had never really enjoyed financial freedom. The goals they had worked so hard to achieve had shimmered away like a mirage. Instead of building their lives, these aims had helped to pull them apart. She wondered how they could have lived differently to avoid the pitfalls they had fallen into.

Like Karen and Jim, are you living in financial bondage? Do you want to be financially free?

If so, I have good news for you! Our wonderful Lord wants you to have enough to provide adequately for your household and to give joyfully and generously to God's work.

Let me share with you nine specific steps you can take to ensure financial freedom for you and your family:

1. Know and obey God's will for your life

2. Breathe spiritually

3. Breathe financially

4. Give regularly

5. Develop a financial plan

6. Budget faithfully

7. Master your credit

8. Create a surplus

9. Invest in God's kingdom

Know God's Will

God's will about money is not a mystery. Biblical principles of stewardship give us a clear revelation of His plan. By basing our decisions on these precepts, we will experience lasting financial freedom.

Every investment of time, talent and treasure, unless otherwise directed by the Holy Spirit, should be determined by the "sound mind" principle of Scripture recorded in 2 Timothy 1:7.

> God has not given us a spirit of fear, but of power and of love and of a sound mind.

Additionally, we should seek the wise counsel of godly, successful people.

There are times in each of our lives, however, when difficult situations arise for which no scriptural principle or human counsel offers specific direction. We wonder,

Which course should I take? How do I know for sure that my decision is right? Even then God makes provision for guidance.

The apostle Paul instructs, "Let the peace of Christ rule in your hearts, since as members of one body you were called to peace."[1] What does this mean?

Peace is a gift and a calling. The Holy Spirit guides us by its presence or its absence in our hearts. When we make the right decisions, we will sense incredible calm even in circumstances that seem impossible. When our actions do not coincide with His plan, however, we will feel restless. Perhaps even churn inside.

No better way exists for us to know God's will in our financial decisions than to base our actions on the principles of His Word, and then to invite the peace of God to guide us from within.

Breathe Spiritually

True financial freedom requires spiritual health.

Earlier I shared how Spiritual Breathing is the secret to living the Spirit-filled life from moment to moment. In Spiritual Breathing, I explained, we exhale the impurities of sin by confession. Then we inhale the purity of righteousness by appropriating the fullness of God's Spirit by faith as an act of the will, inviting Him to direct, control and empower our life.

Good stewardship is a call to supernatural living. No matter how financially wise we may be, we will succumb to material bondage and fruitlessness unless the Holy Spirit controls our life. Unconfessed sin dams the channel of God's blessing. Maintaining short accounts with God through Spiritual Breathing unclogs the flow.

Breathe Financially

As spiritual breathing sustains our spiritual health, so "Financial Breathing" preserves our financial freedom.

We exhale financially by relinquishing the ownership of our resources to God, by surrendering every decision to Him and accepting His direction, and by acknowledging His lordship over all our time, talents and treasure.

We inhale financially by sharing with others the abundance God provides.

This simple act of faith calls for a total, irrevocable commitment to the ownership of God over our lives.

Give Regularly

God did not ask for a tenth of our income or for offerings above our tithes because He needs the money. Rather, He chose giving as a method for securing our financial future.

Our Lord said, "If you will give, you will get! Your gift will return to you in full and overflowing measure, pressed down, shaken together to make room for more, and running over. Whatever measure you use to give — large or small — will be used to measure what is given back to you."[2] By faithfully obeying the biblical principles of stewardship, we enter the flow of heavenly blessing. This enables us to experience godly prosperity.

The first step in this process is to tithe. The apostle Paul instructs, "On every Lord's Day each of you should put aside something from what you have earned during the week, and use it for this offering . . ."[3] When you receive your paycheck, tithe from the top. In so doing, you place yourself under His protection and unlock the windows of blessing.

Outside God's financial covering, we are vulnerable to

Satan's attacks. The enemy delights in draining our resources, thereby robbing us of the ability to further God's kingdom. But our Lord promised, "I will rebuke the devourer for your sakes, so that he will not destroy the fruit of your ground . . ."[4] Faithfulness in tithing brings great reward, for God also promised to "open the windows of heaven and pour out for you a blessing until it overflows."[5]

The second step in the giving process goes beyond the tithe to our offerings. Several years ago, George was praying and meditating about his responsibilities as a steward. "Lord," he asked, "I know the tithe is 10 percent of my income, but how much should I give above my tithe?"

The response, like a thought entering his mind, was immediate and unmistakable, "How much can you trust Me to supply?"

During a missions convention at his church, he decided to put this to the test by pledging a sacrificial amount. Each month for the next year God faithfully supplied the finances for his pledge. Every year George has increased his missions giving, and always God has supplied the needed amount.

Our Lord instructs us to give according to how He blesses us.[6] If He gives us much, we are accountable for much; if He gives us little, we joyfully manage on little. Giving generously or sacrificially beyond our tithe truly honors our Lord.

Develop a Financial Plan

Built upon the foundation of biblical stewardship, financial goals provide the framework for our economic decisions. All Christians do not agree on this issue. Some argue that planning keeps us from relying on God. Others create such rigid plans that they cannot respond to His leading.

Planning, when in balance, reflects the nature of God. The very structure of the universe depends on the intricate order of its elements. If one particle within an atom were to stray from its path around the nucleus, for example, chaos would result. Living without a financial plan also will produce a disastrous effect.

Paul said, "I press toward the mark."[7] A written financial plan gives us a visible target. If prepared according to biblical standards of stewardship, the plan will enable us to measure our progress and stay on track.

Budget Faithfully

Developing a financial plan is not difficult. The family budget serves as a starting point. Easily identifying our needs, wants and desires, the plan provides a vehicle for setting priorities and forming strategic short-range and long-range goals to govern our spending. Furthermore, the budget enables us to think before we buy, thus keeping our spending on target.

The blessings of giving do not give license for foolish spending. Clever advertising and human nature combine for almost irresistible temptation, but living beyond our means inevitably invites disaster.

God will not protect us from the consequences of irresponsible spending just because we tithe. He expects us to live within our means and to be content with the things He provides.

Master Your Credit

Good stewardship requires that we live modestly and effectively manage credit.

Paul admonished, "Pay all your debts except the debt of love for others."[8] Many Christian leaders believe that one should never go in debt for anything. I disagree. A young couple will frequently incur monthly obligations while establishing their home. Throughout life, the purchase of large dollar items — such as a house or a car — usually requires indebtedness. The real danger does not lie in the provision of needs, but in self-indulgence, poor planning, lack of discipline, and the passion to satisfy one's greeds.

Satan aims to drive Christians into debt so he can drain them with worry or despair and keep them spiritually impotent and fruitless. For this reason, a faithful steward will never obligate himself to the place where he cannot, through control of his income, make a reasonable payout.

Marlene and Roy learned this lesson the hard way.

She grew up believing that money would always be available for her every wish. "Nobody ever said no," she remembers. "Even when my parents said there wasn't any more, there always was."

Roy grew up in a family whose affluent lifestyle provided unspoken acquiescence to a similar bottomless-pit philosophy. "There was always enough money," Roy recalls. "If we needed or wanted something, we went and charged it. We didn't shop around; we didn't look for better prices. Only once in twenty-two years did my father caution me against overspending. That day I figured, *Well, he's just in a bad mood.*"

When Marlene and Roy married, their compulsive habits and "easy-come-easy-go" view of money led them to an indebtedness of more than $20,000 that took five years of painful sacrifice to pay off.

Perhaps the apostle Paul had this problem in mind when he said, "No soldier in active service entangles himself in the affairs of everyday life, so that he may please the one who enlisted him as a soldier."[9] Imagine what the results would be if our country were defended by an army too busy with nonessential enterprises to master the basics of military warfare. To be an effective warrior in God's army, we must keep our material resources as free of debt as possible and use them forcefully in the war against Satan. Our lifestyle should reflect the discipline of military readiness for the moment when our Lord summons us into battle.

Create a Surplus

Surpluses seldom happen. We must create them.

Solomon declared, "The wise man saves for the future, but the foolish man spends whatever he gets."[10] Let me suggest a simple formula to accomplish this goal:

Give the first 10 percent of your income to God and save the second 10 percent for the surplus. Then live on the remaining eighty percent.

These percentages may not be possible for everyone. With expenses gobbling all their income, many will find it difficult to save. Creating a surplus demands discipline and a change in spending habits.

You may adjust the amounts for savings and living expenses up or down to suit your needs, but whatever percentage you choose, saving will require sacrifice.

A budget provides an effective tool for this process. My good friend and colleague, Steve Douglass, offers arresting insight in this area. "Interestingly enough," he says, "when I taught financial management to my Sunday school class of college and career-age singles, we found that the single person earning a minimum wage in the state of California probably has more than $100 of monthly surplus over priorities. This simply goes to show that, if we budget our needs very carefully, we will more than likely find ourselves in the very satisfying position of having to decide what to do with the surplus God has given us."[11]

More than a hundred years ago, the famous circuit-riding preacher John Wesley offered sound advice for managing our money successfully. "Earn all you can," he said, "save all you can, give all you can." This simple outline embodies the chief purpose of the surplus: "Give all you can."

Financial emergencies usually hit us when we least expect them. Sometimes a crisis deals a devastating blow. Prudent stewardship compels us to save for such a "rainy day." God wants us to use part of His resources for our families. Even so, the intent of His provision goes beyond our own needs. Paul captured the reason for the surplus in this passage:

> God is able to make it up to you by giving you every-thing you need *and more,* so that there will not only be enough for your own needs, but *plenty left over to give joyfully to others.*[12]

Invest in God's Kingdom

Every Christian should consider how he can give to help win and disciple the largest possible number of people for Christ. If every child of God would do so—whether sacrificially or out of planned abundance—vast sums of money would be available to accelerate the fulfilling of the Great Commission.

I would rather place my confidence in the Bank of Heaven than all the combined financial institutions of the world. No investment—however large or small—pays greater dividends than what we deposit in the treasury of the Heavenly Kingdom.

Perhaps you are wondering, "How can I invest in the kingdom of God? I have no money—just my weekly paycheck, and I must pay rent, buy food and clothing, and take care of many other expenses." By putting God first in your life and applying the principles of stewardship that I have shared with you, you will be able to give. You have God's promise on that.

"But, how much should I invest?" you ask. The amount will not be the same for everyone. It takes both the widow's mite and the wealthy man's abundance to accomplish the work of God. Simply give until you feel satisfied that all the needs He has placed on your heart are met. It is not how much you give only, but how much you have left over after you have given that pleases our Lord.

"How can I give where my investment will do the most good?"

As godly stewards, we must carefully plan to give where the need is the greatest. Oswald Smith asks, "If you see ten men carrying a heavy log, nine of them on one end and one man struggling to carry the other, which end would most need your help? The end with only one man."

Financially, we have the same dilemma in God's kingdom. An estimated 96 percent of all money raised for church budgets stays in America. Sadly, only 4 percent goes overseas to help reach the rest of the world with the gospel. This grieves our Lord, and we cannot expect His blessing as individuals or as the Body of Christ until we obey His command to help fulfill the Great Commission throughout the whole world.

Our generous gifts to foreign missions could help open an entire country or unreached group of people to the gospel. Many who have never heard the name of Jesus nor had the opportunity to read God's Word in their own language could be introduced to our Savior.

I encourage you to ask Him to supply the funds to invest in His work. Look for a special project which you can support monthly, if only modestly, in addition to your com-

mitment to your local church. Prayerfully make a faith
promise commitment that is more than you are capable of
fulfilling according to your present income. Then expect
God to honor this expression of your faith in Him and your
obedience to His command to help fulfill the Great
Commission.

Applying the biblical principles of giving to our time,
talents and treasure provides our greatest security for the
future. No other steps lead to financial freedom and no
other steps lead to the full and abundant life that Jesus
promised to all who trust and obey Him.

For Reflection, Discussion and Action

1. If a fellow Christian asked you for advice on how to handle finances, what would you tell him?

2. Is there any part of your finances that you have not completely surrendered to God? If so, why? How can you give
it over to Him?

3. Why is each of the nine steps to financial freedom vital
to the outcome? Which step is the hardest for you and why?

4. List several ways in which you can share your abundance
with others, in both material and non-material ways.

5. Find one special project you could contribute to by
making a faith promise.

16

"Give While Your Hand Is Warm"

The story is told that monkey hunters in the jungles of Africa use special jars with long, narrow necks to trap their prey. They fill these jars with fruit and nuts and hang them from limbs in trees.

As a monkey swings by, he spies these odd-looking things. Curious, he stops to investigate. Discovering the jar filled with food, he reaches his hand down through the neck and grabs a fistful of goodies.

With his fist clenched around the fruit, however, he can't pull the food out of the jar. No matter how he turns his bulging hand, he cannot slide it up through the narrow neck. Instead of releasing the food, he greedily hangs onto his treasure until the hunter captures him.

We laugh at the foolishness of this monkey risking his life for a bit of food. Yet how many of us act as selfishly with the possessions our Lord has entrusted to us? Instead of releasing our God-given resources into His control, we hang onto them, trapping ourselves in selfishness or greed. As a result, we rob ourselves of the blessings of God.

Handling Your Wealth

Most of you who read this book have good incomes. In comparison to most of the world, the average American could be considered wealthy. We own comfortable homes, two or more cars, nice clothes, and we enjoy many of life's other blessings. Providing adequately for our spouses, children and grandchildren is good stewardship. One does not live prudently in this world without a reasonable amount of insurance to cover medical needs, funeral expenses and provision for those we may leave behind. A good financial plan also will include preparation for retirement.

Some Christians do not stop there, however. Many spend a lifetime building financial security. Having plenty to live comfortably, they continue to accumulate more and more wealth. Like the monkey with his fist clenched in the jar, they hold onto their possessions and trap themselves in a lifestyle of over-accumulation.

Like any of our talents, the ability to make money is God-given. In Deuteronomy, God's Word admonishes, "Always remember that it is the Lord your God who gives you power to become rich."[1] God gives us the ability to gain wealth, not to hoard but to share. The apostle Paul instructs, "If God has given you money, be generous in helping others with it."[2] Since the talent for making money belongs to Him, He holds us accountable for what we do with it. Many neglect their responsibility as stewards and thus indulge themselves in over-accumulation.

Giving While You Live

Since everything we possess actually belongs to God and He has made us temporary stewards, we do not leave *our* money behind when we die; we leave God's money. Then someone else assumes responsibility for our estate. Many Christians work hard and leave their estates to heirs who are unfaithful to the trust. But a faithful steward, after providing for the present and future needs of his family, invests in God's kingdom while he still lives.

Today, while I was editing this manuscript, I spoke over the telephone with a beloved friend of forty years, Louis Evans, Jr. He shared a timeless Hebrew axiom with me: "Give while your hand is warm." Many Christians have discovered their greatest joy and blessing in doing so.

R.G. LeTourneau was such a man. He had a contagious fervor for our Lord. When I knew him, he was in his later years yet still radiated an enthusiasm for Jesus Christ and His kingdom.

God gave LeTourneau the ability to design and build huge construction machinery that enabled him to make tens of millions of dollars. He considered the godly stewardship of his wealth of primary importance.

In 1935, he formed the LeTourneau Foundation to use his resources for the spread of the gospel. Into this foundation, he gave 90 percent of his income. As a result, millions of dollars have gone to train and send men and women around the world to help fulfill the Great Commission. He also inspired many others to invest in God's kingdom.

A Christian friend recently shared how he had been appointed the executor of a sizeable estate and would be responsible to give to Christian ministries the money of a woman after her death. Instead, my friend encouraged her to give the money away while she could observe first-hand the benefits of her investments.

They prayed together, and with his counsel and the help of others, she began to give her money to many worthy Christian projects—to missionaries and mission organizations, struggling new churches, and Christian schools. The results were exciting. As she gave generously, God blessed her abundantly and made the final period of her life the most fruitful.

Not realizing the extent of their stewardship, most Christians give only from their current cash income. At least one Christian financial advisor, however, counsels his clients to tithe periodically on everything they own. I encourage you to give from all your resources, not just from your discretionary income.

Fortunately, the United States government encourages charitable giving through its income and estate tax laws. This allows individuals to make outright gifts of cash, stocks, bonds, mutual funds, real estate or other tangible property.

You can participate in a variety of charitable programs that will help further the cause of Christ without jeopardizing your current income or that of your heirs. I encourage you to consult your attorney, certified public accountant or trust officer for specific information about these plans.

Giving From Modest Means

The principle of giving while we live applies equally to those with modest means as well. Some time ago, a friend came to me for counsel about his investments. "The Lord has blessed me with a steady income," he explained, "but I'm not wealthy. Over the last two years one of my investments has brought an additional income of $10,000. Should I give all of this to the Lord now, tithe on it, or invest it to make additional profits for the Lord?"

I would like to suggest some guidelines for answering these questions:

1. Maintain your present standard of living.

2. Give all or at least half to further the cause of Christ *now*.

3. Should you choose not to give the entire

amount, invest the remainder where *all* the profits go to the Lord. See how much money you can make for Him!

God deals with us individually. I cannot suggest your lifestyle nor give you a specific plan for investing in the cause of Christ. I do urge you to use your resources for the kingdom while you can direct them in the way God leads you. Do not leave this responsibility to your heirs or executors, unless absolutely necessary.

Ministering After Your Death

For every believer in Christ, death is a final triumphant act by which we enter eternally into the presence of our Lord. The apostle Paul speaks of this moment in his first letter to the Corinthians. "When this happens," he said, "then at last this Scripture will come true—'Death is swallowed up in victory. O death, where then is your victory? Where then your sting?'"[3]

Humanly speaking, however, our death is the most difficult reality we experience. Millions of Christians fail to face this certainty. For the steward who walks in the power of the Holy Spirit, death is an opportunity to minister. Through our estate, we can use even more of our resources to help win and disciple men and women for Christ after we are gone.

A will helps us accomplish this purpose. Ron Blue, a dear friend and financial expert, describes a will as "a written, witnessed document that defines your final wishes and desires regarding many things, including property distribution."[4]

A will is essential for several reasons. First, we can provide a final testimony to our faith in Christ. Ron Blue explains, "A will can provide a public record of your Christian testimony, not only for your children but also for anyone else who reads that document, including attorneys, judges, accountants, and perhaps grandchildren, great-grandchildren, and the like. Obviously, without a will, you do not have that public testimony."[5]

Second, a will shows our commitment to godly stewardship. Another dear friend and financial advisor, Lloyd Copenbarger, emphasizes the significance of this record. "I believe it is extremely important that our children and families see that, even in death, our priorities remain constant," he explains. "We should support the Lord's work during our lives and as our last conscious act. The amount of the gift is less important than the fact that it has been made."[6]

Third, a will ensures that what we leave behind is correctly distributed. Without it, the government will divide our estate. Rarely will the state achieve our objectives.

Fourth, a will eliminates many unnecessary expenses and stresses for those handling our affairs. The process of distributing our wealth is simplified and less costly.

Fifth, a will enables us to provide for our heirs. God wants us to make sure our family has enough resources to maintain a reasonable lifestyle after we are gone. Let me give a word of caution, however. We must not overindulge our children. Giving too much to our heirs is a danger many of us never consider. We must help them develop independent and creative lives, not stifle them with too much wealth.

Richard LeTourneau explains his father's philosophy:

> Dad . . . had seen enough cases of what happened to the second generation when they had wealth dumped in their laps, and he wanted to avoid any possibility of this happening in his own family. He had the tremendous insight and wisdom to know that allowing his children to have access to much money, even when they are grown and mature, could be destructive to them if they were not

totally committed to Christ.[7]

Finally, a will can provide for the Lord's work. Many of our assets are not available for the kingdom of God until our death. Through a will, we can continue to help fulfill the Great Commission long after our physical life ends.

Do you have a will? Have you made provision for your family and God's work after your death? Each year hundreds of millions of dollars are wasted in unnecessary taxes and legal costs, simply because many Christians do not leave a will. We must be better stewards of our funds. I urge you to consider prayerfully your priorities. Ask an attorney to help you draft a will. Instruct him to designate a major portion of your estate to those Christian causes which have demonstrated a high degree of integrity and fruitfulness. Review your will periodically and update it as necessary.

Abundant blessings surely come to those who wisely invest their resources to help fulfill the Great Commission. I encourage you to experience the excitement of giving "while your hand is warm." You will see the fruit of your gifts multiply and grow in the lives of others while you are still alive. What a joy to watch your resources touch lost and hurting people around the world!

For Reflection, Discussion and Action

1. In what ways does our culture encourage over-accumulation? What negative results can you note in your area from this emphasis? How has it affected your church?

2. In your own words, explain what the proverb "Give while your hand is warm" means. Explain how it applies to godly stewardship.

3. Have you ever tithed on your net worth? Would this step make a big difference in your giving?

4. If you do not have a will, make an appointment with an attorney this week to initiate the process of drafting one.

5. Make a plan to periodically review and update your will.

17

How to Trust God for Your Finances

As I write, many savings and loan institutions in the United States are treading turbulent financial waters. Worried depositors are pulling their savings from these institutions, causing the S & Ls further losses totalling billions of dollars.

Hoping to relieve the panic, the federal government is having to bail out the insolvent organizations and closely monitor those on the verge.

Meanwhile, the larger S & Ls have placed reassuring ads in newspapers across the country to boost their faltering reputations. "Our resources are over five times the legal requirement," boasts one. "We're twice as safe as federal regulators require," asserts another. Capitalizing on the bad publicity against their competitors, banks have launched campaigns to lure depositors abandoning the S & L ships.

Furthermore, the economic recessions of the 1970s and 1980s have resulted in tens of thousands of successful individuals, couples and businessmen filing for bankruptcy.

These situations exemplify the instability of finances in the world. Yet most people trust in their investments, savings and retirement plans to ensure security and happiness—only to find their hopes dashed when reverses deplete their assets. Others accumulate sizeable portfolios, then worry about their wealth. Many more plunge deeply into debt through unwise investments or uncontrolled spending. All are wasting their lives trying to achieve security in a volatile world.

Our heavenly Father, on the other hand, wants us to enjoy a full, abundant life free from the cares and stresses that confidence in money brings. Rather than trusting in a worldly system that cannot assure our welfare, or relying on our own weak capabilities to provide for our needs, He calls us to depend entirely on Him.

Let me suggest seven basic steps you can take to develop your trust in God for your finances.

1. Recognize that God is worthy of your trust

2. Realize that God wants you to live an abundant life

3. Keep your heart and motives pure

4. Substitute faith for fear

5. Ask God to supply your needs

6. Take a step of faith

7. Keep your faith active

Recognize That God Is Worthy of Your Trust

The first step in the process of learning to trust God is to recognize that He is worthy of your trust. We cannot separate God from His character. He is perfect in truth. The psalmist wrote, "The Lord's promise is sure. He speaks no careless word; all he says is purest truth, like silver seven times refined."[1] The prophet Isaiah proclaimed, "Trust in the Lord forever, for in God the Lord, we have an everlasting Rock."[2] The psalmist wrote, "Trust in the Lord ... then you will live safely here in the land and prosper, feeding in safety. Be delighted with the Lord. Then he will give you all your hearts desires. Commit everything you do to the Lord. Trust him to help you do it and he will."[3] We can count on God to do as He says because the One who created the heavens and earth and who set the laws that govern the universe is more capable of providing for our needs than we could ever imagine. Make Him the foundation of your financial security.

Realize God Wants You to Live an Abundant Life

Those who trust in Him flourish "like trees along a river bank bearing luscious fruit each season without fail ... For the Lord watches over all the plans and paths of godly men."[4]

Our Lord promises to give every obedient Christian an overflowing, joyous life regardless of his financial position. Jesus told His followers, "I came that they might have life; and might have it abundantly."[5] This generous assurance includes financial freedom.

Keep Your Heart and Motives Pure

Trust in God by itself, however, will not enable us to live abundantly. We must also keep our heart and motives pure. Just like a seed planted in dry, packed soil, our faith cannot produce without the right conditions for growth.

In His holy, inspired Word, God promises to bless those who are upright.[6] He delights in those who walk blamelessly.[7] The wisdom of Proverbs declares, "The upright shall have good things in possession."[8] Since our heavenly Father has promised to lead us in wisdom and uprightness,[9] we need only to ask for His help. Earlier we discovered that our motives can deceive us whether in giving or in trusting God for our finances. Any number of impure incentives may divert our aim to put God first in our stewardship. I encourage you to breathe spiritually when motives displeasing to our Lord creep into your heart. Confess these wrongful attitudes, then appropriate the Holy Spirit to help you rely on Him to supply your needs.

Substitute Faith for Fear

One emotion that can undermine our faith and throw us back into financial bondage is fear. When anxiety over the future grips us, we lose the ability to trust God for our needs.

Fear is one of Satan's most powerful weapons. But it was not always so. The most gracious Giver of all good things implanted this instinct in human nature for our preservation. Without it, we would run headlong into danger, foolishly undaunted by peril. Such godly fear also causes us to dread His displeasure, desire His favor, yield to His will, and conscientiously obey His commands. This virtuous fear underlies faith.

Satan, however, has twisted fear into a product of doubt. In the Garden of Eden, God forbade Adam and Eve to eat of the tree of the knowledge of good and evil. Even so, the crafty old serpent made quick work of Eve. "Really?" he asked. "*None* of the fruit in the garden? God says you mustn't eat *any* of it?"[10] Subtly, he led her along the path of doubt until she could no longer resist temptation. Tasting the delicious fruit, she passed it on to Adam. As they ate, the glory of their innocence vanished and they covered themselves in shame. The fear that once kept them from partaking of the forbidden fruit had been distorted by doubt. Human nature would never be the same. Cowering in the presence of God, mankind would hide in naked disgrace.

Since that disastrous encounter, Satan has not changed his tactic. He still says, "Really? Are you sure?" The faithful steward knows this temptation well. As he contemplates the promise of God to supply all his needs according to His riches in glory, the voice of the enemy is quick. "Really? *All* your needs? What about . . . " Without faith in the integrity of God's Word, we are vulnerable to Satan's assault. The dark rays of doubt will penetrate the recesses of our heart until they paralyze us with fear.

Our defense against fear is awesome. Faith, the devil knows, is like an anchor cast into the sea of God's mercy to keep us from sinking into the despair of doubt. One could not say it more eloquently than the poet, "Faith is a grasping of Almighty power; the hand of man laid on the arm of God; the grand and blessed hour in which the things impossible to me become the possible, O Lord, through thee."[11]

"Fear involves torment,"[12] John said. No one is so miserable as the Christian who steps out of union with the Lord Jesus and walks in disobedience to God. Unable to respond in faith to God's voice, he soon succumbs to anxiety and frustration.

By obeying God's will for our lives, however, we substitute faith for our fear. When we actively do His commands, we establish our faith firmly and open our lives to His abundant blessings. Our Lord promises in John 14:21, "The one who obeys me is the one who loves me; and because he loves me, my Father will love him; and I will too, and I will reveal myself to him."

I encourage you to sustain your financial health through "Financial Breathing." Exhale by surrendering your fear and placing your future into His capable hands.

Inhale by putting into action the principles of God's Word for financial freedom.

Ask God to Supply Your Needs

The apostle James observed, "You do not have because you do not ask."[13] Our Lord said, "Ask, and it will be given to you . . . "[14] Faith requires action. Ask God, as an act of your will, to supply your needs. Do not allow emotions or circumstances to hinder your requests.

God doesn't supply our needs automatically. He wants us to ask that we may involve ourselves in the process and glorify Him for the supply. Whatever we ask, according to faith and in harmony with His will, He promises to supply.[15]

There is unlimited power in the name of Jesus to Whom God has given all authority in Heaven and on earth. God wants us to ask Him for *everything,* in Jesus' name. Matthew writes, "You can get anything—ANYTHING you ask for in prayer—if you believe."[16] Jesus said, "Whatever you ask for from the Father, using my name, he will give it to you."[17] What an amazing and wonderful promise!

I encourage you to trust your heavenly Father as the Source of all things, and to relax in the certainty that He will fulfill His promises.

Through the years, I have traveled many millions of miles by air. When I board an airplane, I do not go to the pilot and express fears that he will carelessly let the plane crash. Instead, I take a seat and relax, or share Christ with the person sitting next to me, or occupy myself with reading, studying and writing.

How much more should we trust our heavenly Father who created us and loves us so deeply? What a wonderful privilege to rest completely in Him because we know that He cares for us.[18]

We truly rest in God when we let Him determine the method and timing of our supply. Our patient trust in God enables the Holy Spirit to work out the details in His perfect time.

Let me encourage you to be content with what He provides. Such an attitude rarely finds its way into our materialistic society. Even among Christians, contentment is not often evident. Many believers misunderstand what it means. Contentment is not merely satisfaction with one's position in life. Rather, it is knowing God's plan and living at peace within it. Contentment in the financial sense means living within the resources God gives us, while striving to make the best use of our assets for His glory.

The apostle Paul set a good example. "I know how to live on almost nothing or with everything," he said. "I have learned the secret of contentment in every situation, whether it be a full stomach or hunger, plenty or want; for I can do everything God asks me to with the help of Christ who gives me the strength and power."[19] Whether in prison, poverty or luxury, the apostle accepted his position with grace and gratitude. He praised the Lord regardless of his circumstances.

Take a Step of Faith

Sometimes God requires of us a further step of faith. Dr. Oswald J. Smith had a burning, driving passion "to bring back the King through world evangelization." The entire ministry of his People's Church in Toronto centered on this vision. The high point of each year was the four-week Annual Missionary Convention. To Dr. Smith, raising support for missions was the prime duty of every individual—from the toddlers in the primary department to the college-and-careers, the filing clerks and millionaires, the homemakers and retired seniors.

Each year, he would challenge them to decide on a "faith promise," which they felt God would put into their hands to give to missions above their regular giving — even if they could not see a way in their budget. No one received a reminder, and miraculously each year more than the amount promised came in.[20]

The basis of this concept is faith in God's ability to supply out of His resources what we cannot give out of our own. During a missions convention, a small boy captured the spirit of faith promise giving. Printing his name and address on a faith promise card, he vowed to give twenty-five cents a month for missions. Then across the bottom of the card in uneven block letters, he scrawled: "My daddy will pay this."

A faith promise involves three key principles.

First, it is an agreement between us and God. No one will try to collect.

Second, it is a commitment, not a pledge. Pledges are made on the basis of what we can give out of our own resources.

Third, it is a plan for giving that enables every Christian to have a part in helping to fulfill the Great Commission.

Taking such a step of faith enriches our life beyond measure. It enables us to venture beyond safe boundaries into new territory. It encourages us to believe God for the impossible.

Joyce remembers well her first experience in making a faith promise. A young adult, she was just beginning her career and attending college classes at night. She and her husband were building a modest home, doing much of the work themselves.

Leading the youth and music ministries of a pioneer church, they devoted a large share of their time and finances to help further God's kingdom.

One night during a service when faith promises were being made, Joyce felt led of the Holy Spirit to promise an additional $25 per week. She had just received a raise in salary, but the $25 still represented nearly a quarter of her weekly earnings. Afraid that she could not give that much, she argued with God. But the inner voice was persistent. "Give $25 a week." Even so, she decided to give only $10.

"I had not yet grasped the concept that my heavenly Father was leading me to give in faith," she recalls. "The very next morning the vice president of the organization where I worked called me into his office. He explained that he was giving me a promotion. Then came the words that I still remember. 'In addition to the raise you've just received, there'll be another $10 increase in your weekly salary.' The voice inside me said, 'If you had given more, you would have received more.'"

Since that time, Joyce and her husband have made many faith promises. God has always provided — though not in the same way. "Sometimes instead of additional finances, He reduces our expenses," she testifies. "The important thing is that He provides!"

As your faith in God and His love and trustworthiness grows, let me encourage you to prayerfully make a faith promise — one that is greater than you are capable of fulfilling according to your present income. Take God at His word to supply from His unlimited resources and make a generous faith promise to help fulfill the Great Commission.

Then, expect a miracle! God has promised in His Word: "Call to Me, and I will answer you, and show you great and mighty things, which you do not know."[21] With our faith and trust, we link our finite lives with the infinite God — the God of love, power, wisdom and sufficiency. We tie ourselves into His inexhaustible supply of answered prayer. We become His instruments for changing the world.

Keep Your Faith Active

As you prayerfully wait for Him to honor this expression of your faith and obedience, keep your faith active. Only as we exercise faith will it remain strong. Faith is not a one-time commitment, nor a mere exercise at our point of need. Rather, it is a way of life. Our active and enduring faith proves whether we truly trust God.

Sacrificial giving flows from obedient trust.

At some time in our lives, each of us must give by faith. When we exhaust our resources, God may open an opportunity for us to invest in a worthwhile cause, or He may show us an individual in need.

What, then, shall we do? Remember God's faithfulness and trustworthiness. On that basis, release your faith and keep on giving. Our Lord will never remain in your debt. As we have previously emphasized, if you obey the Lord in your stewardship, "your gift will return to you in full and overflowing measure"[22] and you will live a joyous, abundant life. He will reward your obedience, for faith places you in position for God's continued blessings.

For Reflection, Discussion and Action

1. Review the seven basic steps to trusting God for your finances. Make them a part of your financial stewardship.

2. Which of these steps are weak areas in your life? Why do you find them hard to apply? What could you do to strengthen them?

3. Suppose a new Christian confides in you that he is afraid

to give God control over his checkbook. How would you advise him?

4. Whenever you feel the Holy Spirit's conviction about your stewardship, you have a choice: Breathe spiritually to confess your sin or go on as you are. How would each of these choices affect your life?

5. Are you reluctant to commit yourself to godly stewardship? If so, why?

18

The Adventure of Giving by Faith

A father and his two teenage sons were setting out on a month-long camping trip in the mountains. They had packed their equipment and drawn their map. On the morning they were to leave, each dressed in his hiking clothes with a sense of excitement.

Ready for their big adventure, the boys gathered their gear and hurried out the door. "Boys! Come back here and sit down for a minute," their father called. "There's one more item we need before we start."

The boys looked at each other and groaned. "Oh, Dad!" the older one exclaimed. "We've gone over our plans and equipment several times to make sure we haven't forgotten anything."

"Yes, you've been very thorough," the father agreed. "But what I'm talking about will determine whether our trip will be a magnificent experience or a huge disaster."

"Tell me what it is and I'll go buy one," the younger son joked.

His father laughed, then sobered. "We can't buy it at

any price. There'll be times during our trip when you will
want to turn back. You'll feel so tired you can barely plant
one foot in front of the other. You may have to sleep cold
and wet. Our food supply may run low. Each of us must
firmly resolve to put every ounce of his strength to last
through the month. If we commit all our strength, will and
wisdom to what lies ahead, this trip will be the most thrilling expedition we ever take together."

The boys nodded enthusiastically. "We're willing and
ready!"

"Let's go, then!" the father announced, shouldering
his pack.

We, too, are about to begin an adventure—the adventure of giving by faith. We have equipped ourselves with
the biblical principles of giving. We have charted our course
by God's Word. Let us now dedicate ourselves to apply these
precepts in faithful stewardship.

Contract With the Lord

Vonette and I have never regretted the commitment
we made nearly forty years ago to put God first in our finances. By the spring of 1951, while I was in my senior year at
Fuller Theological Seminary and directing my business interests, we had become increasingly aware that living for
Christ and serving Him was our major goal in life. We had
lived selfishly before becoming Christians, and had been
ambitious and materialistic. Now the Lord had changed us
and had given us a love for Himself and a desire to serve
Him and others. As a result of this awareness, we decided
to sign a contract with the Lord in which we yielded our
lives and all our possessions to Him, including the giving
of our finances. The results of this decision are still bearing generous dividends today.

As part of our agreement, I began to put aside my business enterprises. While growing up on a ranch in Coweta, Oklahoma, I was inspired by my grandfather, a successful oilman. I dreamed of one day going into the oil business myself. Coming to California, however, I began manufacturing fancy foods. Eventually I made enough money through this successful venture to begin an oil leasing, drilling and production business in Oklahoma. God blessed this new venture in an unusual way, and I envisioned making millions of dollars which we could invest in the cause of Christ.

After a few years, however, the ministry of Campus Crusade began to flourish. We remembered our commitment to never seek or accumulate wealth and realized that God had other plans for us. He wanted our lives more than our money and was leading Vonette and me to give our full time to the ministry of Campus Crusade for Christ.

Looking back, I can see how the promise of our Lord recorded in Mark 10:29,30 is being fulfilled in our lives. "Let me assure you," He said, "that no one has ever given up anything—home, brothers, sisters, mother, father, children, or property—for love of me and to tell others the Good News, who won't be given back, a hundred times over, homes, brothers, sisters, mothers, children, and land—with persecutions! All these will be his here on earth, and in the world to come he shall have eternal life."

Had we been able to give $10 million, $20 million or even $50 million to Christian causes, we would have given a modest amount compared to what God has enabled us to be part of today. Our annual budget in Campus Crusade exceeds $125 million, and with a staff of thousands who, like myself, raise their own support, the amounts that have been given to expand this ministry worldwide total hundreds of millions of dollars. Add to these funds the amounts given to the kingdom of God by the millions of people around the world whom our staff have introduced to Christ and discipled into fruitful Christians, and the figures would probably total many billions of dollars.

In addition, with the cooperation of thousands of other ministries and churches around the globe, Campus Crusade is spearheading a comprehensive strategy called New Life 2000* to help reach the billions who have not yet heard about Christ.

The strategy calls for establishing at least 5,000 training centers, including 10,000 "JESUS" film teams, throughout the world by the year 2000. In each area, the training center and film team will be staffed by trained, local Christians to direct a comprehensive outreach of evangelism, discipleship and leadership training.

This worldwide evangelistic thrust will require us to raise at least another billion dollars in the next ten years.

As a result of our commitment to Christ to give up a materialistic lifestyle, Vonette and I personally own little of this world's goods. Yet we have always enjoyed the blessings of God which He promised to all who trust and obey Him. On thousands of occasions we have experienced the faithfulness of God to meet our every need above and beyond our fondest hopes and desires.

The five rented homes we have lived in, for example, have been as nice as or nicer than anything we might have chosen had I been a millionaire—yet we have never sought to live in luxury.

We chose them on the basis of their suitability to provide a more fruitful ministry for our Lord and have rented each on terms which we could afford on our modest income. Even the car we use for personal and Campus

---

* New Life 2000 is a registered service mark of Campus Crusade for Christ, Inc.

Crusade ministry is a gift from a long-time dear friend.

Though we own nothing apart from a few personal effects and a modest pension for the future, I cannot think of a single thing Vonette and I want that we do not have — except more finances and blessings from God to pass on to others.

Our experiences, however, are not unique. Over the years, we have also seen our Lord work in miraculous and powerful ways through the finances of many believers. Let me share with you testimonies of how God has enriched and exhilarated other Christians through their obedience in godly stewardship.

God's Miraculous Accounting

Mark and Ruth wanted to use the money God entrusted to them to help fulfill the Great Commission. As young believers, they had heard someone talk about giving a percentage of income to the Lord and, by faith, increasing the proportion each successive year.

This plan made sense to them. They believed that giving according to God's blessing went far beyond the tithe.

When newly married, they began giving 10 percent to the Lord Jesus. Each year, they increased the percentage.

As they gave more of their income to the Lord, they found it necessary to manage their resources more efficiently. To save money, they asked a representative of the local utility company to check their use of energy and suggest how they could live more economically. Mark took the man around the house for an inspection.

When the man finished his survey, he thoroughly checked their energy bills and receipts from the previous year. Confused, he turned to Mark and Pam. "This is impossible!" he declared. "I don't know how you can heat the house and provide electricity at such a low cost."

For eight years, Mark and Ruth have continued to increase their proportion of giving. During that time, they have added three children to their family and moved to an expensive area of the country. In addition to their other expenses, they now have tuition payments. They still can't explain how God has enabled them to give and make their figures come out right on a ledger. But they have seen God do the impossible with their finances.

Mark explains how confident he feels about using such an unusual approach to giving. "I don't know how far we'll be able to take our plan, but we can say that God has somehow met all our needs and enabled us to give away a lot of money over the years. Numerically, this makes no sense. God has bypassed my accounting!"

A Deposit in a Tree

For some time, Melanie had wanted to step out in faith in her giving. She had never expected, however, to be challenged as clearly as she was one morning in college. As she trudged to her place of work, the message of the speaker in the college chapel whirled through her mind. She barely recalled his face, but his words were so alive to her that she couldn't escape them.

Melanie fumbled with her keys and absentmindedly unlocked the door to the glass-fronted office. Crossing the empty room, she flung the keys onto her desk and sank into her chair.

A frown creased her forehead. *What would posses me to promise a hundred dollars?* she asked herself. She pulled out a stack of work, then leaned back. *I can't concentrate,* she sighed. *How will I ever come up with that much money above my tithe for the missions project?*

Reaching into her purse, she pulled out her checkbook and ran her finger down the list of entries:

Tuition for this semester's classes at college

Car payment

Textbooks and supplies

Tithe to the church

The income from her part-time job barely covered her expenses. How could she manage to carve another hundred from her paycheck to honor her faith promise?

Bowing her head over her work, she prayed in a whisper. "Lord, I was so sure this morning that I had the faith to give that amount. I know You promised to provide. Please show me where to get the money by next month. Thank You for knowing my needs."

The week before her commitment was due, she still had no way to raise the money. As she drove to work, she mentally went over her budget again trying to find some way to cut enough corners. *There's no extra,* she finally concluded.

Parking along the curb, she turned to walk to the office. Something bright caught her eye. Across the street, in a vacant lot, she noticed a white piece of paper in the crook of a tree.

Curious, she crossed the pavement to check it out and discovered a sealed envelope. Examining both sides, she could find no identifying marks.

I wonder who put this here? she mused. Tearing it open, she drew out a hundred dollar bill.

Her hands trembled. *Where could this have come from?* She glanced all around her. *Maybe this money is part of a drug deal.* She could see no one. *What should I do with it now? I can't leave it here.* She turned back toward the office. *I'll just have to locate the owner.*

For the next week, Melanie asked everyone she saw at work if they had lost an envelope. Her boss also mentioned it to his customers. By Friday, he advised her to take the money home. "If no one's come to claim it before now, they never will!" he declared. "I'm sure you can find a good use for it."

Driving back to her dorm that night, she joyfully sang choruses of praise to the Lord. *Thank you, Lord,* she prayed silently. *What a marvelous way to send me the money for my faith promise.* Then she giggled. *A heavenly deposit in a tree — just for me.*

She proudly fulfilled her faith promise that Sunday, bubbling with delight as she described God's "creative banking."

No one ever came to claim the money, and the miraculous incident inspired Melanie to give by faith many times after that.

More Than a Million

Don and Virginia, from rather modest resources compared to the super rich, determined to give $1 million to the cause of Christ. They did not have that kind of money, but believed that God would enable them to give that amount through their new business. With the help of the Lord, they planned to give $50,000 a year for twenty years.

God honored their faith and hard work, and within ten years this dedicated couple achieved more through their business than they ever expected. As a result, Don and Virginia gave more than $1 million to the work of the Lord and held forty evangelistic dinners costing tens of thousands of dollars, at which several thousand guests received Christ.

The Great Privilege of Giving

The joyful and abundant life that our Lord promises to His faithful stewards never ends, for He continually finds creative ways in which to bless us. I never stop being amazed at the miraculous ways He uses us to help others as we put Him first in our finances.

Right now, I am embarking on one of the most exciting adventures in giving of my lifetime. It all started one evening when I turned on the television to watch Dr. Charles Stanley, pastor of the First Baptist Church in Atlanta, Georgia.

He spoke on "God's Formula for Blessing," using a familiar Scripture verse which I have often claimed and taught myself. "If you give, you will get! Your gift will return to you in full and overflowing measure, pressed down, shaken together to make room for more, and running over. Whatever measure you use to give—large or small—will be used to measure what is given back to you."[1]

The first step to God's blessing, he said, is having a lifestyle of giving. Generosity toward the cause of Christ helps us overcome covetousness and is a barometer of spirituality.

As I listened, a thought flashed through my mind. *If I give my pension to establish a New Life Training Center, God will help me raise the money for the rest of the 5,000 New Life Training Centers that have not yet been underwritten.*

I knew of several individuals on our Campus Crusade staff who had received a lump-sum payment of their full pension when they reached the age of sixty-five. Until the moment when I was watching Dr. Stanley, it never occurred to me to draw on my pension. Even though I helped establish our pension plan, I have given little thought through the years to Campus Crusade having one. Listening to Dr. Stanley, I recalled the verse, "For it is God who is at work in you, both to will and to work for His good pleasure."[2] Could He work through me to help set up one of these training centers? I had no idea how much my pension totalled, but covering the cost of one training center would take $50,000.

Joyfully, I considered the prospect.

In what area of the world would the Lord want me to direct my giving? I knew the answer immediately.

Forty-three years ago, I heard Dr. Oswald Smith challenge about a thousand college students and young singles to commit their lives to helping fulfill the Great Commission. He asked each of us to place our name on a country and claim it for the Lord through prayer and finances as God would lead—if necessary, even to give our lives to help reach that country for Christ. I had put my name on the Soviet Union and begun praying for its people.

Two years later, after I married Vonette, she joined me in praying for the Soviet Union. In 1978, at the request of the Soviet church, the government asked us to tour and speak throughout the country. We accepted eagerly and preached the gospel eighteen times in eight cities with fantastic results. Ten years later, we helped to train hundreds of pastors and laymen in the Soviet Union's republic of Estonia. A few months ago, the head of the Protestant leadership in the Soviet Union visited Arrowhead Springs and asked us to start a New Life Training Center in Moscow.

My years of praying for the Soviet people had given me a special love and burden for them. Now, with my pension, I could have a rare opportunity to finance a training center to help reach many of them for our Lord Jesus Christ!

First, though, I had to discuss my plan with Vonette. Although Vonette has her own separate pension plan, whatever I do with my pension affects her, too. After thoroughly listening to my vision and asking a few pertinent questions about her concerns, she responded enthusiastically.

We checked with the finance department at Campus Crusade to find out how much money had accumulated in my pension fund. To our amazement, I had almost the exact amount needed to fund the training center.

Vonette and I discussed the plan further and prayed about our decision, considering our financial security for the future. Since I intend to serve the Lord until my last breath, a plan for leisure retirement holds little significance for me. Vonette and I agreed to trust the Lord to provide for our older years.

Later, I felt impressed to share our decision with the leadership of New Life 2000. I asked Vonette to join me. Together, we eagerly described how God had led us to make this commitment. Joy still floods my heart as I share this story with you.

God reserves a special blessing for those who give generously of their time, talents and treasure to His work. Have you made your commitment to help fulfill the Great Commission through faithful stewardship?

I urge you to develop a personal strategy for giving that will enable you to invest wisely in the kingdom of God and increase your fruitfulness for Christ. Acknowledge God as the source and owner of your possessions, and be ready to give an account of your stewardship to Him. Offer your gifts to the Lord Jesus as an act of praise and worship. Put God first in your giving. And manage your time, talents and treasure to bring glory to His name. In so doing, you too will experience the wonderful adventure of living and giving by faith.

A

How to Help
Change Your World

"I sense God's hand on this most important endeavor. God's people are coming together. So many different denominations and mission agencies are answering Christ's call to unite and get the Good News out quickly. I count it a rare privilege to be involved closely with New Life 2000."

Dr. Ted Engstrom
President Emeritus, World Vision
Chairman, New Life 2000
Committee of Reference

One of the most exciting aspects of the Spirit-directed walk is that we have the matchless privilege and opportunity of helping share the Good News with our world. Have you ever seriously considered how you can help change the world for the glory of God?

Right now, thousands of Christian organizations and churches are teaming up for a comprehensive, ongoing thrust into all regions of the globe to help share God's love and forgiveness with those who do not know Him. The strategy involves millions of obedient Christians from all walks of life—and you can be one of them!

What is New Life 2000?

New Life 2000 is a comprehensive plan for world evangelism—a strategy to help fulfill the Great Commission in obedience to our Lord's command in Matthew 28:18-20. Through this plan every Christian can play a significant role in helping to take the message of new life in Jesus Christ to the entire world by the year 2000.

New Life 2000 links the almost forty years of evangelism and discipleship training of Campus Crusade for Christ with millions of Christians from thousands of churches of all denominations and other Christian ministries, which are committed to helping fulfill the Great Commission.

The strategy of New Life 2000 includes establishing 5,000 ministry areas throughout the world — one center for each population area of approximately one million people. A New Life Training Center, with its tailor-made, culturalized ministry strategy, will be located in each area.

Each New Life Training Center, directed by local national Christians, will coordinate the work of evangelism and discipleship as part of a comprehensive outreach strategy in its area. The strategy includes the use of the "JESUS" film and an ongoing leadership training program, which emphasizes "spiritual multiplication" in accordance with 2 Timothy 2:2.

Within each of the 5,000 areas, we anticipate planting hundreds of New Life Groups, ranging in size from 10 to 30 people, composed largely of new Christians. The groups meet one or more times each week to teach believers the biblical basis for a vital Christian walk and fruitful ministry. In many areas, New Life Groups cluster to form new churches in alliance with existing local churches of various denominations.

(The cost for a New Life Training Center, including staff salaries, equipment, transportation, etc. will average $50,000 per year. Depending on country and culture, the cost will range from $30,000 to $70,000. After three to five years, the centers should be self-supporting by national believers.)

Why is Campus Crusade for Christ launching New Life 2000?

Trained Christians reaching others with the gospel in their own language in every community worldwide, has been at the heart of Campus Crusade for Christ since the ministry began in 1951.

New Life 2000 is not a new plan. It is an acceleration of Campus Crusade's nearly four decades of serving the body of believers, helping them "go and preach the gospel to every creature" and helping new Christians to grow in their personal relationship with God, so that they will, in turn, win and disciple others, generation after generation, through the process of spiritual multiplication.

What are the goals of New Life 2000?

- Present the gospel to more than 6 billion people by the year 2000

- Introduce at least 1 billion people to faith in Jesus Christ

- Involve 200 million new Christians in New Life Groups

- Train millions of leaders through 5,000 New Life Training Centers

- Establish discipleship and training ministries on 8,000 campuses worldwide to help introduce millions of college students and their professors to Christ

- Start 10 million New Life Groups

- Help establish more than 1 million churches in cooperation with thousands of churches of all denominations

- Assist local churches and individuals in adopting one or more of the 5,000 New Life Training Centers at an average cost of $50,000 per center

Who is involved in New Life 2000?

Christians from North America, Europe and more than 150 nations around the world are a part of New Life 2000. These men and women from diverse backgrounds include pastors, students, businessmen, homemakers, diplomats, prisoners, farmers, athletes, executives and military leaders.

Millions of believers within thousands of churches,

denominations, organizations and mission agencies are uniting to make New Life 2000 a priority for their evangelism and discipleship ministries at home and abroad.

The "JESUS" Film

The "JESUS" film, sponsored and financed through Campus Crusade for Christ, and filmed in Israel, is believed to be the most biblically accurate feature motion picture on the life of our Lord Jesus Christ ever produced.

By January 1, 1989, it had been viewed by approximately 330 million people in live audiences, in 128 languages, with 47 languages in process. Tens of millions have already indicated salvation decisions for Christ. The goal of New Life 2000 is to make the "JESUS" film available in 271 major languages, representing every language group of a million or more people, and at least 1,000 dialects.

We are praying for and believing God that more than 1 billion people will be introduced to Christ through this film ministry along with the many other evangelistic efforts of New Life 2000. The film is also effective among students, executives and other specialized groups in North America, as well as among hidden people in Third World countries.

Many churches in North America will be training their members to show the "JESUS" film evangelistically in their homes. For example, Dr. Jack Hayford, pastor of Church on the Way, Van Nuys, California, and his associates are training 1,000 couples to show the "JESUS" film in their homes at least twice each year. They are anticipating that at least 1,000 to 2,000 people will be reached for Christ through this and other evangelistic efforts in their church this year.

Today through New Life 2000, you can know with absolute assurance that your life has counted . . . that you have helped to lead millions of people into Christ's kingdom.

Will you dare to believe God that your partnership in New Life 2000 could help bring the message of Jesus Christ to the whole world by the end of this century?

"It has been my privilege to know Bill Bright and the ministry of Campus Crusade for Christ for nearly 40 years, and for that and other reasons I am happy to serve as honorary chairman of New Life 2000.

"I believe that it is going to be an enterprise that can help touch the entire world for Christ by the end of this century. We are going to be praying and working together, and I hope that you and your church will get behind it and make this one of the greatest evangelistic efforts in the history of the church in modern times."

Dr. Billy Graham
Evangelist
Honorary Chairman, New Life 2000

For more information on how you can be a part of this vital strategy, please write:

Campus Crusade for Christ
Office of Communications (41-50)
Arrowhead Springs
San Bernardino, CA 92414

B

Resources to Help
You Grow and
Share the Good News

For Personal Evangelism

Have You Heard of the Four Spiritual Laws? *Bill Bright.* One of the most effective and widely used evangelistic tools ever developed, the Four Spiritual Laws gives you a meaningful, easy-to-use way of sharing your faith with others. 0-86605-064-7/Pkg. of 50

Would You Like to Know God Personally? A new adaptation of the Four Spiritual Laws, presented as four principles for establishing a personal relationship with God through Jesus Christ. 0-89840-204-2/Pkg. of 50

Witnessing Without Fear. *Bill Bright,* with a foreword by Billy Graham. A step-by-step guide to sharing your faith with confidence. "The chapter on 'Conquering the Fear of Failure' is worth the price of the book," says Ann Kiemel Anderson. Pastor Charles Stanley writes, "If you're praying for an unbelieving friend, neighbor or loved one, this book is for you." Ideal for both individual and group study; a Gold Medallion Award winner. 0-89840-176-3

Reaching Your World. A six-part video/workbook package for Sunday school classes, midweek Bible studies, and visitation or evangelism training. Includes video vignettes and instruction, student workbooks, leader's guide, copies of *Witnessing Without Fear* and evangelistic booklets.

Jesus and the Intellectual. *Bill Bright.* Investigates the claims of Christ and the validity of Christianity from an intellectual and felt-need point of view. *Jesus and the Intellectual* includes Bible verses and a four-point outline of the gospel. It's a useful evangelistic and follow-up tool. 0-86605-071-X/Pkg. of 5

Good News Comic Book (Children). Introduce children to Christ with this colorful gospel story. Children can use it to share with other children. It's an excellent gift for birthdays or holidays. 0-86605-069-8/Pkg. of 25

How to Get Better Grades and Have More Fun (High School and College). *Steve Douglass and Al Janssen.* Here's what every student is looking for: help from a Harvard MBA for getting better grades and spending less time doing it. It gives practical guidance to help all students raise their grade point average, deal with stress and manage their time. Includes a clear presentation of the gospel. Fast reading and easy to apply. 0-89840-090-2

How to Achieve Your Potential and Enjoy Life (Adult). *Steve Douglass and Al Janssen.* Written by a Harvard MBA in the popular style of *How to Get Better Grades and Have More Fun,* this book helps adults who want to find success and fulfillment. Practical, motivational, and with a clear presentation of the gospel. An ideal book to share with your non-Christian friends. 0-89840-184-4

Tell It Often, Tell It Well. *Mark McCloskey.* You can gain confidence and practical help to initiate sharing your Christian faith with others through this motivating and insightful book. It is a well-reasoned, biblical approach to fruitful witnessing, and is used as a text in several Bible colleges and seminaries. 0-89840-124-0

For Personal Discipleship

The Secret. *Bill Bright.* In this honest and easy-to-read book, Dr. Bright presents the process of being filled with the Holy Spirit and keeping Jesus Christ on the throne of one's life. He shares how Christians can live in tune with God's supernatural purposes for their lives. 0-89840-243-3

Personal Disciplemaking. *Christopher B. Adsit.* A step-by-step guide for leading a Christian from new birth to maturity.

Howard Hendricks writes, "This is the most comprehensive, practical approach to one-on-one disciplemaking I have seen." 0-89840-213-1

The First Year of Your Christian Life. *Steven L. Pogue.* Ideal for New Convert classes or for use as a personal gift for a new Christian, this book helps the new Christian understand the essential basics of his walk with Jesus Christ. 0-89840-195-X

Transferable Concepts. *Bill Bright.* These booklets explain the "how-to's" of consistent, successful Christian living. They're great for personal follow-up and discipleship. They are also available as one conveniently bound paperback titled *Transferable Concepts for Powerful Living.*

How to be Sure You Are a Christian
How to Experience God's Love and Forgiveness
How to be Filled With the Spirit
How to Walk in the Spirit
How to Pray
How to Witness in the Spirit
How to Introduce Others to Christ
How to Help Fulfill the Great Commission
How to Love by Faith
How to be an Effective Member of the Body of Christ

Five Steps to Christian Growth. Establishes new believers in five cornerstones of the faith: assurance of salvation, steps to growing, understanding God's love, experiencing God's forgiveness and being filled with the Spirit. 0-91856-33-101 *Leader's Guide*/0-918956-34-X

Ten Basic Steps Toward Christian Maturity. *Bill Bright.* These eleven individual booklets from the *Handbook for Christian Maturity* cover practical, biblical steps to developing your Christian walk.

Introduction – The Uniqueness of Jesus
Step 1 – The Christian Adventure
Step 2 – The Christian and the Abundant Life
Step 3 – The Christian and the Holy Spirit
Step 4 – The Christian and Prayer
Step 5 – The Christian and the Bible
Step 6 – The Christian and Obedience

Step 7 — The Christian and Witnessing
Step 8 — The Christian and Stewardship
Step 9 — Highlights of the Old Testament
Step 10 — Highlights of the New Testament

Transferable Concepts for Powerful Living. *Bill Bright.* This book will give you and your disciples the help you need for a consistent and victorious Christian walk. Previously available only as Transferable Concepts booklets, these lessons are now compiled into one convenient study guide. Discover the ten most important ingredients for enriching your spiritual life and learn ways to pass this vital information on to others. 0-86605-163-5 *Leader's Guide*/0-86605-161-9

Handbook for Christian Maturity. *Bill Bright.* As the follow-up material for the nationwide Power for Living campaign, this book has fostered new life and growth among individuals and study groups looking for help in understanding the Christian life. You'll focus on the ten most essential building blocks for developing a strong walk of faith. 0-86605-010-8

Knowing God's Heart, Sharing His Joy: A 31-Day Experiment. *Dick Purnell.* For all who would like to know and share what is on God's heart, Dick Purnell has prepared thirty-one days of personal Bible study, prayer and practical implementation. You'll discover the burden on God's heart for the world, and then move to the message God has for everyone, especially those who do not have a personal relationship with Christ. 0-89840-219-0

Promises: A Daily Guide to Supernatural Living. *Bill Bright.* A daily devotional guide to help change your life. Live a supernatural life every day by meditating and acting upon God's promises. Now available in paperback. 0-86605-178-3

At Christian bookstores everywhere.

Or call
Here's Life Publishers
1-800-950-4HLP

Notes

Chapter 1: Stewards Over All
1. Mark 16:15 (TLB).
2. John 10:10 (TLB).
3. 3 John 2.
4. Psalm 1:2,3.
5. Psalm 24:1 (NIV).
6. Colossians 1:15-18.
7. 1 Peter 1:18,19.
8. Ephesians 1:20-23.
9. Romans 12:3 (NIV).
10. Acts 17:28.
11. Matthew 25:14-30; Romans 14:12.
12. Mark 16:15; Matthew 28:19.
13. Proverbs 23:7.
14. 2 Timothy 2:2.

Chapter 3: Qualifications of a Steward
1. 1 Corinthians 4:2.
2. 1 John 1:7.
3. John 15:1-8.
4. 2 Timothy 1:7.
5. Matthew 25:14-29 (TLB).
6. Luke 16:10,11.

Chapter 4: Attitudes of a Steward
1. Luke 6:43-45.
2. 2 Corinthians 9:7, *Letter to Young Churches,* a translation of the New Testament Epistles by J.B. Phillips, (New York: The Macmillan Company, 1957).
3. Matthew 5:42.
4. Matthew 10:8; 19:21; Luke 11:41.
5. Matthew 25:33-40.
6. Job 13:15.
7. Matthew 6:33; Colossians 3:2.
8. 1 Thessalonians 5:18 (TLB).
9. 2 Corinthians 9:7 (TLB).
10. Acts 20:35.
11. "Hilarious Giving," *Worldwide Challenge* (November/December 1984), p. 41.

Chapter 5: Responsibilities of a Steward
1. Habakkuk 2:4; Romans 1:17.

217

2. Hebrews 11:6.
3. Jeremiah 23:24.
4. Ephesians 2:4,5.
5. Mark 16:15 (TLB).
6. Matthew 28:19.
7. Ephesians 5:15,16.
8. 1 Corinthians 12:7.

Chapter 6: The Principles of Giving
1. Anonymous.
2. Genesis 8:22.
3. Matthew 5:42.
4. Matthew 10:8.
5. Acts 10:38.
6. Luke 6:38.
7. Luke 6:38.
8. Genesis 1:28.
9. Genesis 22:17.
10. 2 Corinthians 9:10.
11. Matthew 15:32-38; John 6:1-13.
12. 2 Corinthians 9:6-10; Luke 6:38; Galatians 6:7.
13. Mark 1:32-34; 3:10; 6:53-56.
14. John 7:38.
15. 1 Corinthians 15:58.
16. James 2:14-18.
17. 2 Corinthians 9:8 (TLB).
18. Acts 20:35.
19. Proverbs 3:9, 10; 11:24,25; Malachi 3:10; 2 Corinthians 9:6,10,11.
20. Philippians 4:19 (NKJV).
21. 2 Corinthians 8:9 (TLB).
22. Ephesians 2:6; 1:3.
23. Ephesians 1:14.
24. Colossians 1:28.

Chapter 7: The Basis of Giving
1. Galatians 6:7.
2. Genesis 1:11 (TLB).
3. Galatians 6:7,8.
4. Matthew 17:20.
5. Leviticus 22:21.
6. Hosea 10:12.
7. Matthew 25:14-20; Luke 19:12-27.
8. Gerald R. Thompson, "The Biblical Foundation for a Planned Giving Program," an unpublished essay, CBN University, 1987, p. 12.

9. John 12:24 (NKJV).
10. John 12:25 (NKJV).

Chapter 8: The Goal of Giving
1. Matthew 22:37-40.
2. Gensis 1:27,28.
3. 1 Timothy 5:8 (NASB).
4. Ephesians 5:25.
5. Psalm 127:3.
6. Psalm 103:13 (NASB).
7. Matthew 5:13,14.
8. Acts 1:8 (TLB).
9. 1 Corinthians 9:9,14 (NASB).
10. 3 John 6.
11. 2 Corinthians 9:8 (TLB).
12. Galatians 6:10.
13. Luke 12:43 (NKJV).

Chapter 9: Motives for Giving
1. Acts 5:4 (NASB).
2. 1 Samuel 16:7 (NASB).
3. Romans 11:35 (TLB).
4. 1 Timothy 6:5,6 (NASB).
5. 1 John 3:16,17 (NASB).
6. 2 Corinthians 5:9 (TLB).
7. Matthew 25:21 (NKJV).
8. Matthew 6:19-21 (TLB).
9. "Junk That Missionary Barrel," *Moody Monthly* (September 1977), p. 56.
10. Matthew 28:19 (NKJV).

Chapter 10: Addressing the Controversy
1. Galatians 5:18 (NASB).
2. Numbers 18:21,23.
3. Hebrews 7:28 (NASB).
4. John 14:12.
5. Hiley Ward, *Creative Giving* (New York: The Macmillan Company, 1958), p. 63.
6. 1 Corinthians 16:2 (NASB).
7. 2 Corinthians 9:5,7 (NASB).
8. R.T. Kendall, *Tithing* (Grand Rapids: Zondervan Publishing House, 1982), p. 41.

Chapter 11: Tithing: The Historical Foundation
1. Hiley H. Ward, *Creative Giving* (New York: The Macmillan Company, 1958), p. 21.

2. Henry Lansdell, D.D., *The Sacred Tenth* (London: Society for Promoting Christian Knowledge, 1906), pp. 19-20.

3. Ward, *Creative Giving,* p. 25.

4. Lansdell, *The Sacred Tenth,* p. 37.

5. Colossians 1:16; John 1:3 (NASB).

6. Matthew Henry and Thomas Scott, *Logos Commentary on the Bible, Genesis—Deuteronomy* (Plainfield, NJ: Logos International, nd) p. 15.

7. Henry and Scott, *Commentary on the Bible,* p. 15.

8. Genesis 14:17-20.

9. Romans 4:11,12.

10. Genesis 28:20-22 (TLB).

11. Deuteronomy 14:23 (TLB).

12. Deuteronomy 8 and 28; Amos 4.

13. Exodus 22:29,30.

14. Malachi 3:1-12.

15. Matthew 23:23.

16. Luke 18:9-14.

17. Mark 12:30 (NASB).

18. Proverbs 3:9 (NKJV).

19. John 21:25 (NKJV).

20. Luke 20:25 (NKJV).

21. Acts 6:1-3; 11:20-30.

22. 1 Corinthians 16:2 (NASB).

23. Ward, *Creative Giving,* p. 47.

Chapter 12: Tithing in a Modern World

1. B.K. Kuiper, *The Church in History* (Grand Rapids: WIlliam B. Eerdmans Puplishing Company, 1951), p. 278.

2. Henry Lansdell, D.D., *The Sacred Tenth* (London: Society for Promoting Christian Knowledge, 1906), p. 458.

3. Hiley H. Ward, *Creative Giving* (New York: The Macmillan Company, 1958), p. 59.

4. Ward, *Creative Giving,* p. 65.

5. Ward, *Creative Giving,* p. 66.

6. *Emerging Trends,* vol. 9 no. 6, June 1987, Princeton Religion Research Center, p. 4.

Chapter 13: Tithing Your Time and Talents

1. James 1:27; Galatians 2:10.

2. Matthew 6:31-33 (TLB).

Chapter 14: God Wants You to Be Financially Free

1. Luke 12:42,43; 16:10,11.

2. Philippians 4:11.

3. 1 Timothy 6:10 (NKJV).

 4. Proverbs 15:6 (NKJV).
 5. Ecclesiastes 5:19 (NKJV).
 6. Philippians 4:12 (NKJV).
 7. Philippians 4:12 (TLB).
 8. Luke 12:15 (NKJV).
 9. Proverbs 30:8,9 (NKJV).
10. Mark 4:19.
11. Ecclesiastes 5:11,12 (NKJV).
12. Proverbs 27:24 (NKJV).
13. Matthew 6:19 (NKJV).
14. 1 Timothy 6:9 (TLB).
15. John 10:10 (NKJV).
16. Author unknown.

Chapter 15: How to Be Financially Free
 1. Colossians 3:15 (NIV).
 2. Luke 6:38 (TLB).
 3. 1 Corinthians 16:2 (NASB).
 4. Malachi 3:11 (NASB).
 5. Malachi 3:10 (NASB).
 6. 1 Corinthians 16:2.
 7. Philippians 3:14.
 8. Romans 13:8 (TLB).
 9. 2 Timothy 2:4 (NASB).
10. Proverbs 21:20 (TLB).
11. Stephen B. Douglass, *Managing Yourself: Practical Help for Christians in Personal Planning, Time Scheduling and Self Control* (San Bernardino, CA: Here's Life Publishers, 1978), p. 198.
12. 2 Corinthians 9:8 (TLB).

Chapter 16: "Give While Your Hand Is Warm"
 1. Deuteronomy 8:18 (TLB).
 2. Romans 12:8 (TLB)
 3. 1 Corinthians 15:54,55 (TLB).
 4. Ron Blue, *Master Your Money* (Nashville: Thomas Nelson Publishers, 1986), p. 206.
 5. Blue, *Master Your Money,* p. 201.
 6. "Willful Giving," *Worldwide Challenge* (November/December 1984), p. 42.
 7. Richard LeTourneau, *Success Without Succeeding* (Grand Rapids: Zondervan Publishing House, 1976), p. 89.

Chapter 17: How to Trust God for Your Finances
 1. Psalm 12:6 (TLB).
 2. Isaiah 26:4 (NASB).
 3. Psalm 37:3-5 (TLB).

4. Psalm 1:3,6 (TLB).

5. John 10:10 (NASB).

6. Psalm 112:2.

7. Proverbs 11:20.

8. Proverbs 28:10 (KJV).

9. Proverbs 4:11.

10. Genesis 3:1 (TLB).

11. Author unknown.

12. 1 John 4:18 (NKJV).

13. James 4:2 (NKJV).

14. Matthew 7:7 (NKJV).

15. 1 John 5:14,15.

16. Matthew 21:22 (TLB).

17. John 15:16 (TLB).

18. 1 Peter 5:7.

19. Philippians 4:12,13 (TLB).

20. Lois Neely, *Fire in His Bones: The Official Biography of Oswald J. Smith* (Wheaton, IL: Tyndale House Publishers, 1982), pp. 232-33.

21. Jeremiah 33:3 (NKJV).

22. Luke 6:38 (TLB).

Chapter 18: The Adventure of Giving by Faith

1. Luke 6:38,39 (TLB).

2. Philippians 2:13 (NASB).